D1101566

PREVENTION OF
BLACK ALCOHOLISM

PREVENTION OF BLACK ALCOHOLISM

ISSUES AND STRATEGIES

Edited by

ROOSEVELT WRIGHT, JR.
Ph.D.

Associate Professor
Graduate School of Social Work
The University of Texas at Arlington
Arlington, Texas

THOMAS D. WATTS
D.S.W.

Associate Professor
Graduate School of Social Work
The University of Texas at Arlington
Arlington, Texas

CHARLES C THOMAS • PUBLISHER
Springfield • Illinois • U.S.A.

Published and Distributed Throughout the World by
CHARLES C THOMAS • PUBLISHER
2600 South First Street
Springfield, Illinois 62717

© *1985 by* CHARLES C THOMAS • PUBLISHER
ISBN 0-398-05139-9

Library of Congress Catalog Card Number: 85-4786

With THOMAS BOOKS *careful attention is given to all details of manufacturing and
design. It is the Publisher's desire to present books that are satisfactory as to their physical
qualities and artistic possibilities and appropriate for their particular use.* THOMAS
BOOKS *will be true to those laws of quality that assure a good name and good will.*

Printed in the United States of America
Q-R-3

Library of Congress Cataloging in Publication Data
Prevention of black alcoholism.

   Includes bibliographies and indexes.
   1. Alcoholism--United States--Prevention. 2. Afro-
Americans--Mental health services. I. Wright,
Roosevelt. II. Watts, Thomas D. [DNLM: 1. Alcoholism--
prevention & control--United States. 2. Blacks.
WM 274 P9443]
RC565.P73   1985   362.2'927'08996073   85-4786
ISBN 0-398-05139-9

Dedicated to

My brother John Arthur Wright, and his family, and my father, Alphonso, and mother-in-law, Janie Simmons

and

Rebecca Anne and Jeanine Lisa Watts

CONTRIBUTORS

CREIGS BEVERLY, Ph.D.

Dean and Professor
Atlanta University School of Social Work
Atlanta, Georgia

SETHARD BEVERLY, M. Div.

Doctoral Candidate
St. Paul's Theological Seminary
Kansas City, Kansas

CARANN SIMPSON FEAZELL, M.S.S.W.

Coordinator, Employee Assistance Program
Southwestern Bell Telephone Company
Dallas, Texas

THOMAS C. HARFORD, Ph.D.

Acting Chief
Epidemiology Branch, Division of Biometry and Epidemiology
National Institute on Alcohol Abuse and Alcoholism
Rockville, Maryland

BARBARA LYNN KAIL, D.S.W.

Assistant Professor
Graduate School of Social Work
The University of Texas at Arlington
Arlington, Texas

SHIRLEY WESLEY KING, PH.D.

Associate Professor
Graduate School of Social Work
The University of Texas at Arlington
Arlington, Texas

RAYMOND SANCHEZ MAYERS, PH.D.

Associate Professor
Graduate School of Social Work
The University of Texas at Arlington
Arlington, Texas

JOHN S. McNEIL, D.S.W.

Associate Professor
Graduate School of Social Work
The University of Texas at Arlington
Arlington, Texas

CAROLYN F. SWIFT, PH.D.

Stone Center for Developmental Services and Studies
Wellesley College
Wellesley, Massachusetts

THOMAS D. WATTS, D.S.W.

Associate Professor
Graduate School of Social Work
The University of Texas at Arlington
Arlington, Texas

MILLREE WILLIAMS

Staff Writer
Alcohol Health and Research World
National Institute on Alcohol Abuse and Alcoholism
Rockville, Maryland

ROOSEVELT WRIGHT, JR., PH.D.

Associate Professor
Graduate School of Social Work
The University of Texas at Arlington
Arlington, Texas

INTRODUCTION

PROBLEMS ASSOCIATED WITH alcoholism and alcohol abuse among black Americans have been repeatedly documented in the literature (Harper, 1979; King, 1982; Watts and Wright, 1983). This literature has consistently suggested that alcoholism is a debilitating psychological and emotional problem (Harper, 1976; Kane, 1981; Royce, 1981), a major public health problem (Harper, 1976; Beauchamp, 1980), and an explosive and ignored social problem (Larkins, 1965). Over the past few decades social scientists, governmental policymakers, and others have shown an increasing interest in the prevention and treatment of this immense problem (Moser, 1979). This interest appears to stem, in part, from a recognition and conscious acceptance by society of its responsibility for eliminating and alleviating conditions associated with alcoholism among blacks. In effect, our social system, in an attempt to become more humanistic and responsive to the needs of black Americans, has begun to initiate policy and programmatic efforts aimed at preventing the development or continuation of this problem. We should note, however, that despite the increasing public attention to alcohol problems among blacks, forces against the continuation of this thrust are enormous and active, not the least of which is the current political and economic climate (Reaganomics). Changes in ideological and philosophical commitments and vociferous cutbacks in prevention funding have taken their toll on future programmatic developments. For the most part, the ultimate determination of alcoholism prevention efforts in black communities will take place in the political arena.

The notion of developing and implementing systematic programs to prevent black alcoholism presupposes deliberate and orchestrated efforts that build appropriate coping and adaptive strengths in black individuals, families, and communities, that promote the growth and development of the entire black community, and that eliminate or ameliorate those environmental conditions that tend to reinforce alcoholism, rather than alleviate it. To accomplish these objectives appropriately, however, will require a conscious recognition of the manifest and latent human potential that exists in black communities, a recognition that they have unique social, ideological, and phil osophical values, and a genuine sensitivity to their collective cultural characteristics. We submit that the newly found interest in the prevention and treatment of alcoholism among blacks is a movement in the right direction. Unfortunately, this movement is still more at the idea level than the political and funding level. We hope that these will conjoin in the future.

When the severity of the problem of alcoholism among blacks is considered, it is surprising that such a paucity of research exists on the prevention of black alcoholism. Of the research that is available, much of it is descriptive and/or based on subjective and anecdotal information (Miranda, 1983). Since the mid-seventies however, more empirically-based studies on black alcoholism prevention have begun to appear, though still far from short of being enough. The emergence of this growing body of research, in effect, is the major impetus for the development and publication of this book. We think that there is a need now for a book that brings together in one volume the best of what we know at the present time about the prevention of alcoholism among blacks. Thus our main purpose for developing this book is to provide a book that compiles and creatively synthesizes information about alcohol prevention and education in black communities. A second purpose of this book is to meet the needs of social scientists, policymakers, educators, public health professionals, social workers and others who are increasingly involved in working with black alcohol abusers, their families, and their communities. We feel that the existing literature has much to offer in respect to initiating policies toward preventing alcoholism in black communities.

The conception of *prevention* that shapes this book is one that reaches beyond the boundaries of several disciplines and professions. As it is used in this book, alcoholism prevention refers to deliberate courses of action taken by individuals, families, and communities that are aimed at changing or ameliorating harmful drinking practices (NIAAA, 1981). The reasons for stressing this particular conception of prevention are pragmatic and theoretical. We think that since drinking is a normal experience in life, the goals of preventive efforts should be most logically directed at increasing the likelihood that individuals who do drink develop drinking behaviors that are personally and socially acceptable.

The focus of this book is on *prevention*. We feel that it makes common sense to attempt to prevent alcohol abuse and alcoholism prior to signs or symptoms of problems, at which point it becomes necessary to treat it. We recognize, however, that alcoholism can be prevented from continuing once it has been detected. The focus on prevention, we submit, is a pertinent orientation for understanding and dealing with alcoholism in black communities as we embark into the 1980's.

MODELS OF PREVENTION

In the public health field, the concept of prevention has been divided into three distinct levels: primary, secondary, and tertiary. Tertiary prevention refers in a general way to treatment, secondary prevention refers to early identification of at-risk populations and appropriate interventions, while primary prevention involves altering the individual or the environment (e.g., aid the individual or environment in developing conditions by which alcohol abuse and alcoholism problems are reduced so that the injurous social, emotional, and physical effects of alcohol are no longer destructive) (Watts and Wright, 1983). It is probably safe to say that policies in the field of alcohol and alcoholism have predominately developed along tertiary prevention lines, with beginning but relatively weak attempts at secondary prevention and virtually no efforts whatsoever in the area of primary prevention. Substantiation for this view is given by Wilkinson, who notes that "experts on drinking problems have often talked of the need for prevention, but when it comes to detailed, rigorously thought-out proposals, they have had much more to say about treatment, about attempts to cure people who already have drinking disorders" (Wilkinson, 1970:4). It appears that this is true of alcoholism efforts with both white and minority populations.

Our conception of black alcoholism prevention is parallel to our conception of black alcoholism, that is, we view black alcoholism as a complex environmental, physiological, health and mental health problem (Watts and Wright, 1983). Any prevention effort(s) therefore, must, in a responsive manner, address the wide ranging complexity of the problem.

A careful review of the literature on alcoholism prevention indicates that current approaches to prevention have been derived mainly from five major theoretical frameworks. The *proscriptive model* views any alcohol use as problematic and proposes abstinence as the only viable prevention strategy (Blane, 1976). This model was dominant during the Prohibition Era and is still influential in certain religious groups. The *socialization model* posits that alcohol problems result from inaccurate information and faulty attitudes and values regarding alcohol. Prevention efforts based on this model attempt to increase knowledge and change attitudes and values to promote responsible decisionmaking about alcohol use (Stallcup et al., 1979).

A third theoretical framework is the distribution of consumption model, based on research which indicates a direct relationship between the level of alcohol consumption in a population, the prevalence of heavy drinking, and the rates of certain alcohol-related problems (Schmidt and Popham, 1978). Proponents of the control model advocate stabilizing or reducing per capita consumption by restricting the availability of alcohol (Dawkins, 1983).

A fourth theoretical framework for prevention is the *public health model* which proposes that three factors interact to produce health and social problems: the host, the agent, and the environment (U.S. Department of Health, Education, and Welfare, 1978). In alcohol problems, the host is the individual drinker, the agent is alcohol, and the environment is the physical and sociocultural setting in which drinking decisions are made and in which drinking occurs. Prevention efforts try to change the host's behavior, the exposure to the agent, and/or environmental influences so that alcohol-related problems will be reduced (NIAAA, 1982).

A fifth framework, the *sociocultural model*, emphasizes the relationship between alcohol problems and the normative patterns of alcohol use within a society (Blane, 1976). It attempts to explain variations in alcohol-related behaviors as functions of such factors as social class, sex, place of residence, and race (Pittman, 1980). Variants of this model place further emphasis on relationships between behaviors and structural factors (Jessor and Jessor, 1980), social norms (Room, 1981), psychological processes, attitudes, person-environment interactions, cultural values, beliefs, and traditions (Harford, 1980; Beverly, 1983; Watts and Wright, 1983). Some proponents of the sociocultural model believe that alcoholism prevention measures must modify and/or eradicate patterns of belief and behavior about alcohol and its use, and oppressive and hostile systemic arrangements (i.e., proactive prevention policies and programs to change, modify, and measurably reduce the sources of oppression in society) (Beverly, 1983; Benjamin and Benjamin, 1981).

Reflection upon the frameworks presented above suggests that it is important to distinguish between at least two major categories of prevention measures: (1) those which attempt to persuade people to do something or refrain from doing something and which attempt to deter drinking or behavior associated with it and (2) those which attempt to shape the environment or situations within which drinking and the problematic events associated with it occur (Gusfield, 1982). Implicitly and/or explicitly these frameworks recognize that alcoholism prevention measures must be designed to influence as much of the total environment as possible. The pathogenesis of black alcoholism is intimately rooted in psychological, biological, environmental, and sociocultural phenomena. As a result, approaches to public policy and preventions based on viewing alcoholism as a unitary phenomenon will be ineffective and inappropriate. That is, undue attention to any one arena of alcoholismic behaviors to the neglect of others can only lead to fragmented approaches to both prevention and treatment. Thus, eclectic approaches to the prevention of alcohol-related problems among blacks are necessary if we are to alleviate the configuration of factors contributing to an individual's abuse of alcohol (Stimmel, 1984). Prevention approaches must, therefore, be comprehensive in nature, promote responsible drinking behaviors and, at the same time, reduce the psychological and social damages associated with inappropriate usage (Miranda, 1983; NIAAA, 1981).

The disaggregation of black alcoholism into distinct components allows for the consideration and development of specific and targeted prevention strategies. For example, we might develop consumption control policies that reduce the social risk of alcoholism (e.g., minimum age drinking laws, taxation policies and limitations on retail outlets). At the same time, we might target prevention approaches at the family, interpersonal, and community mores, values, and attitudes toward drinking behavior (e.g., churches, social and recreational programs, education programs, etc.). What is eminently clear from available data is that no singular prevention approach is likely to be optimal. We are convinced that a combination of diverse prevention strategies must be employed (e.g., coordinated approaches that regulate supply, legal and educational approaches to drinking practices, and interventions in the environment).

ORGANIZATION OF THE BOOK

This book is divided into two major parts. Part I is oriented toward the difficult problem of explicating and synthesizing major paradigmatic models of alcohol use and abuse among blacks. The chapters included in this part tend to focus on analyzing, discussing major theoretical perspectives and conceptual approaches to prevention. The authors of the various chapters discuss some of the major strengths and weaknesses of contemporary prevention models, measures, and strategies that have been designed specifically for blacks. In addition, attention is given to delineating viable directions for the future in planning prevention activities and programs for blacks who abuse alcohol.

A recurrent theme presented in these chapters is that a comprehensive analysis of alcoholism among blacks is difficult at this time because of: (1) the lack of systematic research on this population; and (2) the lack of models that take into consideration cultural factors in examining, treating, or preventing alcohol abuse. These factors make it difficult to plan and develop prevention and treatment programs or social policies that effectively impact blacks who are alcohol abusers, their families and communities, and society as a whole.

Finally, Part II includes a series of chapters which examine issues associated with alcoholism and its prevention among black subgroups. We feel strongly that a comprehensive analysis of alcohol use and alcoholism among blacks must be sensitive to differences between males and females, differences in respect to socioeconomic background and status, and differences between geographical settings with their very different environments. The chapters in Part II take into consideration these timely concerns. They provide readers with knowledge gained through carefully conducted investigations concerning the etiology of alcoholism as well as consideration of prevention ideas in respect to black subgroups, and the black population as a whole. Without a sound understanding of subgroup differences, it is virtually impossible to develop appropriate prevention policies and programs. Indeed, we would argue that those interested in the problem of alcoholism among blacks need a comprehensive compendium of research-based information to guide the planning, development, and implementation of successful program models. To this end, we offer this book as a beginning step toward the development of a prevention orientation to the problem of black alcoholism.

REFERENCES

Beauchamp, D.E.: *Beyond Alcoholism: Alcohol and Public Health Policy.* Philadelphia, Pennsylvania, Temple University Press, 1980.

Benjamin, R., and Benjamin, M.: Sociocultural correlates of black drinking: Implications for research and treatment. *Journal of Studies on Alcohol* (Suppl. 9): 241-245, 1981.

Beverly, C. C.: Psychosocial research and its application to alcohol and drug addiction programs. In Watts, T. D., and Wright, Jr., R. (Eds.): *Black Alcoholism: Toward a Comprehensive Understanding.* Springfield, Illinois, Charles C Thomas Publs., 1983, pp. 184-197.

Blane, H. T.: Education and the prevention of alcoholism. In Kissin, B., and Begleiter, H., (Eds.): *Biology of Alcoholism,* Vol. 4. New York, Plenum, 1976, pp. 519-578.

Dawkins, M. P. Policy issues. In Watts, T. D., and Wright, Jr., R. (Eds.): *Black Alcoholism: Toward a Comprehensive Understanding.* Springfield, Illinois, Charles C Thomas Publs., 1983, pp. 206-220.

Gusfield, J. R.: Prevention: Rise, decline and renaissance. In Gomberg, E. L., White, H. R., and Carpenter, J. A. (Eds.): *Alcohol, Science and Society Revisited.* Ann Arbor, Michigan, The University of Michigan Press, 1983, pp. 402-425.

Harford, T. C. Theoretical synthesis: Discussion, In Harford, T. C., Parker, D. A., and Light, L. (Eds.): *Normative Approaches to the Prevention of Alcohol Abuse and Alcoholism.* Washington, D.C., U.S. Government Printing Office, 1980, pp. 171-196.

Harper, F. D.: *Alcohol Abuse and Black America.* Alexandria, Virginia, Douglass Publishers, 1976.

Harper, F. D.: *Alcoholism Treatment and Black Americans.* Rockville, Maryland, National Institute on Alcohol Abuse and Alcoholism, 1979.

Jessor, R., and Jessor, S. L.: Toward a social psychological perspective on the prevention of alcohol abuse. In Harford, T. C., Parker D. A., and Light, L. (Eds.): *Normative Approaches to the Prevention of Alcohol Abuse and Alcoholism.* Washington, D.C., U.S. Government Printing Office, 1980, pp. 37-46.

Kane, G. P.: *Inner-city Alcoholism: An Ecological Analysis and Crosscultural Study.* New York, Human Sciences Press, 1981.

King, L. M.: Alcoholism: Studies regarding black Americans, 1977-1980. In National Institute on Alcohol Abuse and Alcoholism. *Alcohol and Health Monograph 4., Special Population Issues.* Washington, D.C., U.S. Government Printing Office. DHHS Publication NO. (ADM) 82-1193. Printed, 1982, pp. 385-410.

Larkins, J.: *Alcohol and the Negro: Explosive Issues.* Zebulon, North Carolina, Record Publishing Co., 1965.

Miranda, V. L.: Black alcohol prevention programming-past, present, future. In Watts, T. D., and Wright, R., Jr. (Eds.): *Black Alcoholism: Toward a Comprehensive Understanding.* Springfield, Illinois, Charles C Thomas Publs., 1983, pp. 162-173.

Moser, J.: *Prevention of Alcohol-Related Problems: An International Review of Preventive Measures, Policies and Programmes.* Geneva, World Health Organization, 1979.

National Institute on Alcohol Abuse and Alcoholism. *A Guidebook for Planning Alcohol Prevention Programs With Black Youth.* Rockville, Md., 1981.

National Institute on Alcohol Abuse and Alcoholism. *Alcohol and Health Monograph 4., Special Population Issues.* Rockville, Md., 1982.

Pittman, D. J.: *Primary Prevention of Alcohol Abuse and Alcoholism: A Critical Analysis of the Control of Consumption Policy.* Unpublished paper delivered at the 26th International Institute on the Prevention and Treatment of Alcoholism, Cardiff, Wales, Scotland, June, 1980.

Room, R.: Case for a problem prevention approach to alcohol, drugs and mental problems. *Public Health Reports, 96(1):* 26-33, 1981.

Royce, J. E.: *Alcohol Problems and Alcoholism: A Comprehensive Survey.* New York, The Free Press, 1981.

Schmidt, W., and Popham, R. E.: The single distribution model of alcohol consumption: A rejoinder to the critique of Parker and Harman. *Journal of Studies* on Alcohol, 39(3): 400-419, 1978.

Stallcup, H., Kenward, K., and Frigo, D.: A review of federal primary alcoholism prevention projects. *Journal of Studies on Alcohol, 40*: 943-968, 1979.

Stimmel, B.: The role of ethnography in alcoholism and substance abuse: The nature versus nurture controversy. *Advances in Alcohol and Substance Abuse, 4(1)*: 1-8, 1984.

U.S. Department of Health, Education, and Welfare. *Third Special Report to the U.S. Congress on Alcohol and Health*, Noble, E. P., (ed.), DHEW Publ. No. (ADM) 79-832. Washington, D.C., U.S. Government Printing Office, 1978.

Watts, T. D., and Wright, R., Jr.: *Black Alcoholism: Toward a Comprehensive Understanding*. Springfield, Illinois, Charles C Thomas Publishers, 1983.

Wilkinson, R.: *The Prevention of Drinking Problems*. New York, Oxford University Press, 1970.

ACKNOWLEDGMENTS

EVERY BOOK has a unique history which lies beneath its pages. This book is no exception. The thinking and insightfulness of many individuals provided the impetus for editing the present book. We wish to express our thanks to all the contributors. Their experiences and scholarly work have increased our understanding of black alcoholism prevention and has made this book possible.

A number of secretaries have helped in the preparation of the final manuscript. We would like to thank the following people for their much appreciated help: Joy Crow, Carol Davis, and Kathleen Shea. Each of these secretaries made our tasks a lot easier.

While we are obliged to acknowledge the help of all those listed above, we take full responsibility for the strengths, weaknesses, omissions, or commissions of this book.

CONTENTS

PART I
TOWARD FORMULATING BLACK ALCOHOLISM
PREVENTION APPROACHES

PREVENTION OF
BLACK ALCOHOLISM

Part I
TOWARD FORMULATING
BLACK ALCOHOLISM
PREVENTION APPROACHES

PART I IS DEVOTED TO a consideration of the formulation of black alcoholism prevention approaches. There has been, within recent years, an emerging focus on prevention on the part of many legislators, educators, clinicians, practitioners, researchers, and others who are seeking ways to reduce alcohol-related problems and to decrease the personal, social, and economic costs associated with them among blacks. This focus has made it not only necessary to examine the characteristics and full dimensions of black alcoholism but has also highlighted the need to have available reliable, and accurate data on the nature and extent of alcoholism among this group. Otherwise, the task of targeting prevention efforts within this group will be difficult if not impossible.

Any discussion and consideration of prevention approaches designed specifically for blacks must begin with the community or subsociety in which and for which prevention activities might take place. Bloom (1981: 50) states that the first stage of prevention activities is that of "orientation," which involves the overall perspectives toward a perceived problem, value questions, political questions, and the like. Heller, Price, and Sher (1980: 304) discuss the notion of the "prevention target," and ask the following two questions:

> What specific risk situation or population at risk will be studied?
>
> What is the evidence for the risk potential of the particular situation or the evidence for the suspected vulnerability for the group at risk?

Hollister (1976: 41) notes that: "Humility is the keynote in setting the goals of prevention programs." So as we begin our consideration of an overview of black alcoholism in this section, we need to remind ourselves that the history of the study of black alcoholism is quite short. We still know relatively little about it, at least when compared with the enormity (and complexity) of the problem. But thanks to scholars that are represented in this section (and throughout the book) we know more about it now than ever before.

Whereas the introduction to this book focused on a general overview of black alcoholism and prevention, Part I is devoted to a consideration of several prevention models that might be useful in respect to preventing black alcoholism. It could be said that approaches to the prevention of alcohol abuse and alcoholism have been derived from three seminal models: the public health model, the "distribution of consumption" model, and the sociocultural model (National Institute on Alcohol Abuse and Alcoholism, 1981: 104-107).

Part I begins with "Blacks and Alcohol: Significant Dates." There are other dates that could be listed, but this listing provides some key dates in the history of American black alcoholism that help to set a backdrop for this section and the book. The reader should also consider the special reports on alcohol and health published over the years by the National Institute on Alcohol Abuse and Alcoholism (1971, 1974, 1978, 1981, 1984) as helpful background material, as well as other books on black alcoholism (Watts and Wright, 1983), black alcoholism treatment (Brisbane and Womble, 1985), transcultural perspectives on the human services (Wright, et. al., 1983), alcohol abuse prevention (Miller and Nirenberg, 1984), social thought on alcoholism (Watts, 1982; *Journal of Drug Issues*, 1985), the "politics of alcoholism" (Wiener, 1981), and related areas in the health and mental health fields.

McNeil and Wright (1983: 212-213) state that the mental health status of ethnic groups "must be assessed within the framework of their culture and community, as well as their community's relationship to the larger society." Black alcoholism is a multifaceted health and mental health problem (and as well an economic, social, and societal problem) occurring within a particular historical and cultural context. Before beginning prevention efforts, then, one could well utter this dictum rather loudly: "Know the community context." Needs assessment, prevention programs, etc., cannot begin before the community context is understood, and understood well. A Community Assessment Profile is a useful and systematic approach to systematically gathering information about community needs and resources (Sundel, 1983: 237). Along with this, one can also be systematic and comprehensive about analyzing the black community in a total context — that total context includes the context of white America, that total context includes the role of the U.S. liquor industry (Gibson, 1978) (largely owned by a relatively small group of white-owned corporations, with some middle-class black intermediaries serving in various capacities), and other components.

King (1983: 241) states: "Those in the greatest need, yet possessing the least power and means of improving their quality of life, tend to get the most ineffective responses from society." Black alcoholics certainly fit into this category. The Chapters in Part I are dedicated to the goal of explicating the dimensions of black alcoholism. Our goal here is to first gain an understanding of the full dimensions of black alcoholism, so that we might move from there toward effective policies and programs aimed at black alcoholism prevention.

Chapter 1, "Blacks and Alcoholism: Issues in the 1980s" by Millree Williams, discusses the findings of an important workshop on black alcoholism sponsored by the National Institute on Alcohol Abuse and Alcoholism, held in Jackson, Mississippi in 1981 (Williams, 1981: 2). It was fitting that this workshop was held there, because of the Interdisciplinary Alcohol and Drug Studies Center at Jackson State University, Jackson, Mississippi. Williams noted (1982: 2) that at that time it was the only comprehensive alcohol and drug studies program at a historically black college in America. This workshop focused on some of the important issues in black alcoholism in the 1980s. Williams discusses some of the key ideas expounded at this workshop, and in so doing provides a wide-ranging issues landscape for a consideration of prevention models.

Chapter 2, "Prevention of Alcohol-Related Problems: Strategies and Activities," discusses the public health model, the distribution of consumption model, and the sociocultural model, and several prevention demonstration projects that help to bring theory into practice in this area. Interestingly, there has not been much contact between alcohol beverage control boards and alcoholism prevention or treatment programs, highway safety agencies, and departments of public safety. People interested in prevention, it is argued here (among other points) must try to achieve better interagency communication and cooperation.

Chapter 3, "An Analysis of Models of Alcoholism and Prevention and Their Applicability to American Blacks" by John S. McNeil, discusses the public health model, the sociocultural model and the distribution of consumption model, and their appropriateness and applicability in respect to black alcoholism. He notes that a workable model addressing the complexity of black alcoholism must address societal, cultural, psychological, and economic factors, and to date no workable, comprehensive model has been developed that addresses all of these dimensions in a holistic way. Still, several promising steps toward prevention have been made despite the lack of such a model, and the models discussed here do contain some useful insights.

Chapter 4, "The Limitations of Prevention in Addiction Services" by Creigs Beverly, discusses the notion that prevention itself is insufficient, and that the goal of intervention should be social development. Prevention in this respect is seen as necessary to achieve in pursuit of social development as a goal. Prevention, then, is seen here not as an end in itself, but as a means to an end. Beverly discusses prevention as a concept, followed by a discussion of social development in relation to prevention, theories pertaining to the etiology of alcoholism, and finally a discussion of the importance of synthesizing the continuum of prevention to social development. These ideas, he avers, can be applied to other areas of the human services in addition to alcoholism services.

Consideration of the ideas discussed by the authors of the chapters in this section help us to move in a more holistic, systems direction in respect to black alcoholism prevention efforts. We can think of this process as a venture in "societal learning" (Watts, 1981) about this complex problem. Somehow, the complexity of the problem itself seems to dwarf any "model" that some might purport can help us better understand the problem. But, again, this is not a stopping place but a beginning place — we have just begun to learn about preventing black alcoholism (and have barely begun to act on what we have learned). We do need more sensitive and sophisticated research on this problem (National Institute on Alcohol Abuse and Alcoholism, 1984: 129). But we also need more concerted action in the form of sound, well-developed policies and programs that address the prevention of black alcohoism in forthright ways. The chapters in this section provide us with insights in respect to moving us in the direction of the formulation of well-designed black alcoholism prevention policies and programs that can address black alcoholism prevention in comprehensive and effective ways.

REFERENCES

Bloom, Martin: *Primary Prevention: The Possible Science.* Englewood Cliffs, New Jersey, Prentice-Hall Inc., 1981.

Brisbane, Frances L., and Womble, Maxine (Eds.): *Treatment of Black Alcoholics.* New York, Haworth Press, 1985.

Dawkins, Marvin P.: *Alcohol and the Black Community: Exploratory Studies of Selected Issues.* Saratoga and Palo Alto, California, Century Twenty One Publishing, Div. of R and E Research Associates, 1980.

Gibson, D.P.: *$70 Billion in the Black.* New York, MacMillan Publishing Co., 1978.

Heller, K., Price, R.H., and Sher, K.J.: Research and evaluation in primary prevention: Issues and guidelines. In Price, R.H., Ketterer, R.F., Bader, B.C., and Monahan, J. (Eds.): *Prevention in Mental Health: Research, Policy, and Practice.* Beverly Hills, California, Sage Publishing Co., 1980, pp. 285-313.

Hollister, William G.: Basic strategies in designing primary prevention programs. In Klein, Donald C., and Goldston, Stephen E. (Eds.): *Primary Prevention: An Idea Whose Time Has Come.* Proceedings of the Pilot Conference on Primary Prevention, April 2-4, 1976. Rockville, Maryland, National Institute of Mental Health, 1977, pp. 41-48.

Journal of Drug Issues, vol. 15, no. 1 (Winter, 1985). Special issue on "Social Thought on Alcoholism."

King, Shirley Wesley: Service utilization and the minority elderly: A review. In McNeely, R.L., and Colen, John N. (Eds.): *Aging in Minority Groups.* Beverly Hills, California, Sage Publishing Co., 1983, pp. 241-249.

McNeil, John S., and Wright, Jr., Roosevelt: Special populations: Black, hispanic, and native American. In Callicutt, James W., and Lecca, Pedro J. (Eds.): *Social Work and Mental Health.* New York, The Free Press, Div. of MacMillan Publishing Co., Inc., 1983, pp. 175-216.

Miller, Peter M. and Nirenberg, Ted D. (Eds.): *Prevention of Alcohol Abuse.* New York, Plenum Press, 1984.

Morgan, Patricia A.: The political economy of drugs and alcohol: An introduction. *Journal of Drug Issues, 13*: 1-7, 1983.

National Institute on Alcohol Abuse and Alcoholism. *First Special Report to the U.S. Congress on Alcohol and Health.* Rockville, Maryland, 1971.

National Institute on Alcohol Abuse and Alcoholism. *Second Special Report to the U.S. Congress on Alcohol and Health.* Rockville, Maryland, 1974.

National Institute on Alcohol Abuse and Alcoholism. *Third Special Report to the U.S. Congress on Alcohol and Health.* Rockville, Maryland, 1978.

National Institute on Alcohol Abuse and Alcoholism. *Fourth Special Report to the U.S. Congress on Alcohol and Health.* Rockville, Maryland, 1981.

National Institute on Alcohol Abuse and Alcoholism. *Fifth Special Report to the U.S. Congress on Alcohol and Health.* Rockville, Maryland, 1984.

Rubington, Earl: *Alcohol Problems and Social Control.* Columbus, Ohio, Charles E. Merrill Publishing Co., 1973.

Schaefer, J.M.: Ethnic and racial variations in alcohol use and abuse. In National Institute on Alcohol Abuse and Alcoholism: *Alcohol and Health Monograph No. 4: Special Population Issues.* Rockville, Maryland, 1982, pp. 293-311.

Sundel, Martin: Conducting need assessment in a community mental health center. In Bell, R.A., Sundel, M., Aponte, J.F., Murrell, S.A., and Lin, E., (Eds.): *Assessing Health and Human Service Needs: Concepts, Methods and Applications.* New York; Human Sciences Press, Inc., 1983, pp. 234-249.

Watts, Thomas D., and Wright, Jr., Roosevelt (Eds.): *Black Alcoholism: Toward a Comprehensive Understanding.* Springfield, Illinois, Charles C Thomas, Publisher, 1983.

Watts, Thomas D.: *The Societal Learning Approach: A New Approach to Social Welfare Policy and Planning in America.* Palo Alto and Saratoga, California; Century Twenty-One Publ., Div. of R and E. Research Assocs., 1981.

Watts, Thomas D.: Three traditions in social thought on alcoholism. *International Journal of the Addictions, 17*: 1231-1239, 1982. The reader may also be interested in seeing (same author): The uneasy triumph of a concept: The 'disease' conception of alcoholism. *Journal of Drug Issues, 11*: 451-460, 1981; Social thought on alcoholism: Some introductory comments. *Journal of Drug Issues, 15*:1-2, 1985. One of the most interesting and though-provoking books to appear in recent years here is: Beauchamp, Dan E.: *Beyond Alcoholism: Alcohol and Public Health Policy.* Philadelphia, Temple University Press, 1980.

Wiener, Carolyn.: *The Politics of Alcoholism: Building an Arena Around a Social Problem.* New Brunswick, N.J., Transaction Books, 1981.

Williams, Millree: Jackson State program focuses on minorities. *NIAAA Information and Feature Service,* April 1, 1982, p. 2. Published by the National Institute on Alcohol Abuse and Alcoholism, Rockville, Maryland.

Williams, Millree: Workshop addresses black alcoholism issues. *NIAAA Information and Feature Service*, October 28, 1981, p. 2. Published by the National Institute on Alcohol Abuse and Alcoholism, Rockville, Maryland.

Wright, Jr., Roosevelt; Saleebey, Dennis; Watts, Thomas D.: Lecca, Pedro J.: *Transcultural Perspectives in the Human Services: Organizational Issues and Trends.* Springfield, Illinois, Charles C Thomas, Publisher 1983.

BLACKS AND ALCOHOL: SIGNIFICANT DATES

1619 First blacks brought to Virginia colony.

1700 Triangular trade routes use liquor in trade for slaves.

1730 Era of tavern as place of social intercourse.

1750 Laws restricting alcohol use by blacks enacted.

1774 Boston Massacre — Crispus Attucks, drunken sailor, killed.

1778 Black church, African Methodist Episcopal (AME), begins.

1800 Anti-slavery movement begins.

1823 Founding of Liberia — first back-to-Africa movement.

1831 Nat Turner's revolt increases restrictions on blacks drinking, using firearms, and learning to read.

1832 Abolitionist movement led by sober people.

1865 Black codes enacted, restricting use of alcohol and possession of arms.

1879 First migration of blacks to American West.

1906 Death of Paul Lawrence Dunbar, known alcoholic and famous writer.

1914 Beginning of black migrations north.

1920 Prohibition and Jazz Age — era of speakeasies and Harlem Renaissance.

1933 Repeal of Prohibition.

1950 World Health Organization and American Medical Association recognize alcoholism as a disease.

1963 Maryland Public Accommodations Bill enacted.

1966 National commission recommends public health approach to alcoholism.

1970 Comprehensive Alcohol Act authorizes Federal funds for alcoholism treatment.

1975 Increasing awareness of alcoholism as a black community problem.

1980s Beginning of prevention strategies in black communities.

From: *A Guidebook for Planning Alcohol Prevention Programs With Black Youth,* 1981. Courtesy National Institute on Alcohol Abuse and Alcoholism, Rockville, Maryland.

Chapter 1

BLACKS AND ALCOHOLISM:
ISSUES IN THE 1980s

MILLREE WILLIAMS

THERE IS considerable evidence that alcohol problems have a major impact on black Americans. The violent consequences of alcohol abuse have been extreme for black Americans (especially black males) in terms of homicides, accidents, criminal assaults, and other conflicts with the law (NIAAA 1978). In addition, black Americans suffer disproportionately from the health consequences of alcoholism, including cancer, obstructive pulmonary disease, severe malnutrition, intestinal disaccharidase actions, hypertension, and birth defects. The rate of hypertension, higher among blacks than any other group, is further complicated by drinking, according to the Fourth Special Report to the U.S. Congress on Alcohol and Health (NIAAA 1981). It also points out that although cirrhosis mortality rates have generally declined each year since peaking in 1973, they are still disproportionately high among black Americans. In some cities, rates among black males aged 25 to 34 are as much as 10 times higher than for white males of the same age. Overall, the cirrhosis mortality rate for black Americans is nearly twice that of white Americans.

From: Alcohol Health and Research World, vol. 6, no. 4 (Summer, 1982), pp. 31-40. Courtesy of National Institute on Alcohol Abuse and Alcoholism, Rockville, Maryland.

King (1982) suggests that in 1980 alcohol abuse remained "the number one health problem in the black community." He reports that the picture has not improved since 1976 and that no real breakthrough is in sight, either at the level of national social commitment or definitive social science activity. In regard to the severe social consequences of alcoholism in the black community, an NIAAA report (1978) notes that "some researchers attribute the apparently disproportionate devastation caused by alcoholism in the black community to the widespread 'ghettoization' and victimization of blacks in the United States."

Compounding the situation is the fact that blacks are proportionately underrepresented in the service delivery system, both as clients and as caregivers. Black alcoholics and problem drinkers are unlikely to seek out traditional treatment programs unless there is a crisis or mandatory need, such as lifethreatening illness, threat of job termination, or referral by the court or social service agency, according to those in alcoholism treatment settings.

In addition, there has been little recent activity in the research area regarding etiological factors and the social and biomedical consequences of alcoholism unique to the black American. Evidence indicates that drinking patterns among blacks differ from those of whites, and that incidence patterns also differ. But little further research has been conducted in the past five years.

At an NIAAA-sponsored workshop held in Jackson, Mississippi, in the summer of 1981, more than 25 black alcoholism program administrators, educators, and researchers convened to discuss these and other alcohol-related issues facing the black community in the 1980s. Abraham Kidane, California State University, pointed out that in the 1960s and early 1970s there was a gradual improvement in the socioeconomic conditions affecting blacks, with the enactment of the Civil Rights bill (1964) and equal employment opportunity legislation (1972), and the implementation of numerous income maintenance programs. Kidane said that "in the 1970s, we seemed to have lost our momentum in areas of employment and relative income. During the 1974 recession, blacks lost their jobs at double the rate experienced by whites, and as recovery got underway they were called back at a slower rate. Between 1975 and 1978, unemployment remained almost unchanged. In 1969, only 5 percent of all black

women in the labor force and who were heads of families were unemployed; by 1978, the unemployment rate among this group was
up to 15.4 percent.

Kidane linked fluctuations in the economy to the rate of alcohol
problems in the black community, noting that blacks are proportionately more severely affected by economic downturns. Increases in
the unemployment rate, he observed, "have the most significant impact . . . on stress variables." These variables — such as suicide
rates, state mental hospital and prison admissions, homicide, cirrhosis of the liver, cardiovascular and renal diseases, and mortality —
can be correlated with factors like the unemployment rate, he said.

Kidane and other workshop participants agreed that alcohol-
related problems among blacks continue to be a major problem, and
that resources are inadequate to successfully prevent and treat the
problem. There was wide-ranging discussion of the unique differences — historical and cultural — that characterize alcohol problems among blacks, and the need for research, prevention, and
treatment that recognizes the special needs of the black alcoholic.

RESEARCH FINDINGS

Many of the workshop participants echoed Kidane's emphasis,
suggesting that social and cultural factors have a greater impact on
both the etiology and the treatment of alcohol problems among
blacks than is the case among other groups.

"Successful role performance in the black community can rarely
be understood in the absence of factoring into one's analysis the
direct relationship between socioeconomic forces that most often
negatively impact the black communities and the resultant intrapsychic processes of its residents," said Dr. Creigs Beverly of Atlanta
University School of Social Work. He asserted that a psychosocial
model of alcoholism in fact "blames the victim" for social dysfunctioning, and suggested there is "greater promise" in fighting substance abuse in the black community by applying a "sociopsycho-
model," that is, examining how socioeconomic conditions impact intrapsychic (internal mental) processes.

Dr. R. A. Winbush of Vanderbilt University suggested that race and racism are important intervening variables in alcoholism among blacks but noted a lack of research dealing with such variables. In an analysis of reviewed literature on black alcoholism for a 30-year period (1939-1969) done by Harper and Dawkins (1976), only 77 of 16,000 studies dealt with blacks. And of the 77 studies, 66 compared blacks with whites; only 11 examined blacks only. Winbush also observed that researchers prefer comparative studies over longitudinal studies. "Virtually no longitudinal studies exist that measure the long-term effects of services provided to participants of treatment programs," he noted.

Winbush suggested that this paucity of research is damaging, in that there exists little empirical support for the need for treatment programs tailored to special needs of blacks. He suggested that one area of research for the 1980s should address reasons why blacks do not use existing alcoholism service programs. "Even though attrition rates are one of the most vexing problems facing alcoholism service programs, little research exists that precisely identifies factors that contribute to the high dropout rate of blacks in such programs," says Winbush.

Research, the group agreed, is essential if blacks are to be more effectively served by alcoholism programs. There was also consensus that one to encourage such research is to encourage historically black colleges to develop strong research training programs. According to Winbush, black colleges should strength curricular efforts in two areas: a service delivery curriculum for students interested in counseling and treatment of black alcoholics, amd a research track to train black students interested in developing sound data on black alcoholism. Winbush added that "equal numbers of students should be recruited for both tracks, and the program should emphasize career opportunities for each curriculum." There was consensus that greater support for such programming should be sought from both the public and the private sectors.

APPLICATION OF RESEARCH TO TREATMENT

Research, no matter what its intent, has no value if not applied to real-life situations. According to the workshop participants, black alcoholism professionals and those researching alcohol-related data in the black community must find ways of developing stronger partnerships. Just as research must not be divorced from the realities of the program setting, prevention and treatment programs must attend to the need to document their effectiveness through evaluation research. Bertha Holliday, of George Peabody College, pointed out that planners should make prevention outcomes more practical and quantifiable to the extent that they represent indicators of reductions in the negative behavioral consequences of drinking. According to Holliday, this approach should result in more powerful documentation of program effectiveness, which, in turn, would be more amenable to the tight cost-benefit analyses of the '80s. According to Holliday, a pragmatic approach dictates that greater emphasis must be placed on three issues:

- Conceptions of problems and issues
- Role of research
- Selection of program evaluation criteria

As this translates into strategies for black alcohol prevention efforts, it means taking sociocultural and developmental consideration into account when conceptualizing alcohol-related behaviors and their prevention, developing research-based approaches to service provision, and incorporating program evaluation criteria that emphasize indicators of reductions in the negative behavioral consequencs of drinking.

TREATMENT APPROACHES

Workshop participants voiced support for continuing efforts to refine counseling approaches that are "culture specific." Erma Wright of A.L. Nellum and Associates in Atlanta noted that counseling from a cultural perspective has existed since the beginning of counseling. It basically involves understanding the client's frame of reference and incorporating it into therapeutic strategies to maximize their effectiveness. Most of the major therapeutic philosophies are based in the cultural context of the majority of the clients seen by the particular theorist. For example, Freud would not have been successful had he not based his concepts of human behavior on young Viennese women, his primary clients. But would Freud have been successful in psychoanalyzing an African native woman? Most likely no more so than an African witch doctor would be in shouting to a young Viennese woman, even though both the African and Viennese women may manifest the same symptoms. It's the approach that tells the tale.

Conventional alcoholism counseling in this country, not surprisingly, is based in the culture of the majority of clients — white males. Such an approach is not always responsive to the black client's mores and value system. Wright suggested that there is a very basic link between culture and counseling. "If cultures are characterized by their behaviors and learned problem-solving techniques, and if counseling is a process to help the client engage in these very things, it would seem that the two concepts are intrinsically linked," said Wright. "Any discussion of alcoholism treatment and counseling approaches as they relate to blacks must take place in the context of the minority culture — its history, strengths, values, attitudes, and culturally specific treatment approaches."

Wright suggested that, as programs are asked to do more with less, one approach should be to emphasize cultural relevance, in order to maximize program utilization by the primary target group and ensure that existing services are as effective as possible. For programs designed to serve blacks, this means instilling in counselors an awareness that the alcoholism among clients is not problematic, but symptomatic. To address this, according to Wright, counselors must adopt nontraditional roles, i.e., become social change agents. Counselors must work with clients to change the socioeconomic structure that gives rise to some of the problems associated with black clients' poverty, unemployment, poor housing, and poor nutritional habits. "The social change agent role represents a better and more productive use of resources of counselors than a palliative effort to patch up the mistakes of the past without preventing the mistakes from recurring," said Wright.

Wright suggested that counseling from a cultural perspective should incorporate cultural rapport-building actions, including developing treatment strategies and counseling techniques that take into account cultural perspectives about eye contact, touching, time, language, social distance, and other patterns of behavior and communication styles. In addition, a holistic approach should be taken in seeking to understand the black client in the context of family, community, and origin.

REACHING BLACK ALCOHOLICS

Employee Assistance Programs (EAPs) have been highly successful in reaching problem drinkers early in the development of alcoholism. Because early intervention is particularly difficult to accomplish with the black alcoholic, do EAPs offer hope? As with community-based counseling programs, black clients referred by EAPs seem to be underrepresented.

William Rosemon of the Texas AFL-CIO Workers Assistance Program pointed out his experience with black unionists, who constitute approximately 17 percent (2.5 million) of the nation's 13.9 million members. He suggested that blacks generally do not get involved in the politics of labor movements. A major step toward bringing in programs that are sensitive to their concerns would be to increase black participation in union politics, according to Rosemon.

In addition to black inactivity in the political process, Rosemon suggested that there are several other reasons for black unionists' underutilization of treatment services:

- Inability to absorb costs when not included in insurance coverage
- Few black service providers on EAP staffs
- Programs oriented to white middle class
- Few blacks on policy-making committees for EAPs

William Davis of the Little Rock, Arkansas, Office of Alcohol and Drug Abuse Prevention suggested that, with particular regard to black-owned businesses and businesses with a large black employee pool, many of the employers are not as knowledgeable about the advantages of EAPs for their employees as they as should be. "It is imperative that employers begin to look at what makes their employees tick." He suggested that strategies be developed that get employers to look not only at employee performance but at "other significant factors, such as cultural or racial problems that may be operating that will definitely affect that employee's performance." To effectively work with a large black constituency within the labor force and to strengthen, increase, and maintain employee productivity and relations, Davis feels that white and nonwhite employers should consider setting up culturally-relevant programs in the company to increase understanding of the following: black culture and its effect on the black psyche and job performance; interactions between supervisors and employee, especially the white supervisor and black employee; significant problems that often face black employers and employees and the role of industry in helping employees deal with them; and the manifestations of external stress on the black male.

Reaching black alcoholics in rural areas is a particularly difficult problem. In urban areas, prevention treatment and services are available, but underutilized. However, many blacks still live in very rural settings, and the problem of underutilization is compounded because facilities are scarce and less accessible, and drinking patterns have not been documented. The conspicuous absence of documentation concerning alcoholism among rural blacks was a major concern of the conference participants. Some pointed out that one reason for the paucity of research is that alcoholism among rural blacks has no significant social or commercial impact.

Is Alcoholics Anonymous (AA) a viable treatment alternative for blacks? Although blacks have been generally underrepresented in AA, the combination of fewer dollars for programs and increased scrutiny of program effectiveness is forcing blacks to take a longer, harder look at alternatives. Like mainstream treatment programs, AA was founded and traditionally has served primarily the middle-class white male. However, Fulton Caldwell of NIAAA pointed out that there is nothing intrinsically discriminating about AA, and that there are several aspects that, when scrutinized, should be very attractive to blacks fighting alcoholism. According to Caldwell, unlike the analytic mode used in some treatment programs, the focus of AA is on the experiential mode of inquiry. By focusing on the individual's experience with alcohol, AA attempts to validate a person's knowledge via experience. In addition, the essential elements of AA philosophy — sharing of common experiences, mutual acceptance of one another as human beings, and trusting a "higher power" — are all strong elements in the black frame of reference. AA describes itself as a "loose federation of somewhat diverse groups whose unity lies in their primary purpose to achieve sobriety, but whose culture, format, values, composition, and language usage may be quite varied." According to Caldwell, there are AA groups that are predominately black, gay, women only, men only, physicians, lawyers, airline pilots, and numerous other subgroups. The one thing that they all have in common is that they are singleminded in pursing sobriety.

Caldwell suggested that black-oriented treatment programs should consider working more closely with AA. "Since AA has been the most effective program in achieving sobriety, and is the most economical (free), then a very useful resource is being underutilized by a significant portion of the alcoholic population," says Caldwell. AA offers many advantages, Caldwell noted, in that it provides ready access to the AA fellowship, it facilitates a strong followup contact in the aftercare program, it provides a wide variety of sober role models for newer clients undergoing outpatient treatment, and it serves as a "bridging" group to the community for clients undergoing inpatient treatment.

PREVENTION APPROACHES

No major disease has ever been eradicated without a broad-based approach incorporating both treatment and prevention. Reaching today's black youth is the key to the solution of tomorrow's alcohol abuse and alcoholism problems in the black community. According to Valetta Miranda of the Naional Clearinghouse for Alcohol Information, most of today's prevention efforts are geared to youths aged 5 to 18, with a special focus on those in grades K-6. It is during this period when they "are still gathering information that later will be the foundations for attitudes and behaviors," says Miranda. "Many successful youth prevention programs have developed strategies to change the behavior and attitudes necessary to lessen the incidence of alcohol-related problems," she commented. "Such strategies attempt to help youth in looking beyond their present situation and to help them focus on the broader issues of life," says Miranda.

Miranda outlined two strategies for prevention efforts: alcohol-specific and nonspecific strategies. Alcohol-specific strategies address the problem of alcohol abuse directly by trying to influence what people drink and how much, how often, when, why, and where. These strategies have included alcohol education in the school, peer alcohol educator programs, public awareness campaigns, DWI prevention activities, and even training of bartenders to expand their helping role as listeners and referral sources for all types of problems. Nonspecific strategies are designed to affect alcoholism and drinking behavior indirectly, dealing not with alcohol but with the broader aspects of life, such as alternative to drinking and facilitating interpersonal relationships. Many of these activities revolve around values clarification, decision-making and coping skills development, assertiveness training, vocation training and job-finding skills, nonjudgmental interaction between youths and adults, and alternatives for relaxation, such as sports, recreation, and yoga. The more recent comprehensive approaches to alcohol abuse prevention attempt to incorporate both types of strategies to maximize effectiveness. According to Miranda, there are three major program concepts or models developed with NIAAA funding currently being used in different variations across the country.

- Model 1, being tested in King County, Washington, tries to promote positive self-image as a deterrent to alcohol abuse by training teachers to conduct open-ended education sessions in grades K through 12. The classroom sessions address alcohol information, values clarification, self esteem, coping skills, and peer pressure.
- Model 2, the CASPAR program of Somerville, Massachusetts, encourages interaction between youth and adults to identify a structure for appropriate drinking behavior. The program involves training teachers and school counselors to conduct open-ended alcohol education workshops in grades 3 through 12, training peer leaders to conduct supervised activities among peers and other youngsters, and community outreach and education efforts.
- Model 3, at the University of Massachusetts (Amherst), uses

the university community to effect overall cultural and community drinking norms at multiple levels: individual, affiliate group, and the entire campus community. The activities range from training dormitory counselors and conducting peer-led workshops to media campaigns and influencing school alcohol policies.

Although they all lend themselves very easily to culture-specificity, the models were not targeted as demonstration projects to minorities.

Because so little research has been done on prevention for black youth, many of the exercises, models, and strategies were developed by professionals who have worked with youth, have backgrounds in black history, or are experienced in the social problems and issues facing the black community today. Many of these professionals have suggested that future prevention efforts geared toward black youth emphasize the importance of black history and culture, build positive self-concepts, emphasize survival skills, demonstrate sensitivity to the special issue of adolescence, and provide a balance between specific and nonspecific strategies.

The NIAAA's Clearinghouse, said Miranda, has been working to stimulate interest in prevention programming among black churches. As part of this effort, a Guidebook for Planning Alcohol Prevention Programs with Black Youth has been developed as a resource for managers planning prevention services for black youth. The Guidebook encourages the use of community support groups in the prevention effort, based on the belief that the indigenous helping groups in the black community are an untapped prevention resouces. Church organizations, for example, have always been a stable force in the community and responsive to the needs of black youth, says Miranda.

EXPANDING THE RESOURCE BASE

Dr. Lois Chatham, acting associate director for Program Operations of NIAAA, discussed the shift from categorical to block grant funding, reporting that the administrator believes the block grant approach will "permit individual states to assume a larger role in assessing their own health needs and in establishing the priorities that will enable them to meet these needs most effectively." According to Chatham, the administrator also indicated that the new format will give state and local health authorities "the flexibility to respond to new and changing conditions . . . to adjust their programs to local conditions to a greater degree than nationwide requirements have permitted in the past." Chatham said that this new flexibility should offer greater efficiency and cost effectiveness by eliminating duplication among programs, and should maximize the impact of federal dollars by allowing the federal money to be combined with existing state appropriations to further statewide goals. Chatham suggested that alcoholism programs will have to begin to consider alternative funding resources, and that this will require that program priorities are clear and the case for funding these priorities is strongly made. Establishing a consensus on general aims and setting priorities in the area of alcoholism among blacks, she said, is an important first step for programs seeking to serve the black community in making the block grant approach work.

Working with State Government

John Bland, of the Maryland Alcoholism Control Administration, noted that it is important for black providers to develop close working relationships with state governments. Black-oriented programs are relatively new to the alcoholism field, he observed; most have been established in the past ten years, and most have been funded primarily by the federal government and consequently have not established strong ties to the state in which they operate.

Bland commented, "I believe that the agenda for black alcoholism programs today is to survive. Working with the state government, including both executive and legislative branches, is now and increasingly will prove to be important strategy to ensure the continuation of black alcoholism programming," he said.

Bland suggested that no plan to secure funds for program operation will be maximally effective unless strategies are developed that nurture relationships with the state alcoholism authority, state legislature, state health policymakers, statewide prevention network, and the voluntary sector. Bland suggested that, in seeking a share of state funds, service providers become the "squeaky wheel" in order to "get the grease."

When working with the legislature, one needs to pay particular attention to three areas: self-interest, explicit detail, and time, according to Bland. "Politicians understand very well vested interest." He advised program people not to be embarrassed to directly and openly state their case. In presenting the program's case, managers must pay careful attention to details such as program operation, characteristics of population served, facts, figures, and a thorough, documented understanding of the problem, he said. Program managers must know the answers to numerous questions, such as, What is the target population? How many did you treat last year? Are they staying sober? Are they working? How do your services for them differ from others? How much does it cost, and can you do it more cheaply?

"If you have a black state legislative caucus, determine its general effectiveness. If it has a health committee, cultivate the chairperson," advised Bland, "by determining his or her track record on alcohol issues and, where necessary, raise his or her consciousness of the importance of alcohol issues."

Working with both the state legislature and the SAA, suggested Bland, involves a major time investment, a thorough analysis of the issues, and coordination of numerous local and statewide activities. It is also very important to get black representation and input on any of the state health policy-making boards, says Bland.

Regarding prevention, Bland suggested establishing a network (if one is not already in place) that can distribute informational materials available from the federal level to secondary schools and colleges and universities. In addition, program managers should investigate the existence of black alcoholism task force, EAPs in major industries with a large black work force, and the SAA's statewide prevention network.

Local Government

According to Bernard Redd of the Center for Multicultural Awareness in Arlington, Virginia, building networks of professionals and consumers is a big factor in working effectively with local or regional governments and institutions. Understanding the continuum of health care service delivery is very important when working with local governments, said Redd.

"With the passage of the Comprehensive Alcohol Abuse and Alcoholism Prevention, Treatment, and Rehabilitation Act and the Comprehensive Drug Abuse Prevention, Treatment, and Rehabilitation Act, there was a marked change in national policy from supply reduction (law enforcement, seizure) to demand reduction (treatment, prevention, rehabilitation). Local jurisdictions began to experience the benefits of resources for research demonstration studies and training through a federally-planned and coordinated program," said Redd. Yet, because planning guidelines for local agencies were vague, and minority communities were slow in getting involved, early state plans, according to Redd, were not always reflective of minority needs.

These two factors, combined with a lack of data on blacks and alcoholism, placed local planners and managers in the position of developing program strategies that did not always reflect the true needs of the minority communities, said Redd. This contributed to underutilization of treatment, prevention, and rehabilitation services by the target group. Consequently, black programs often have not grown from a community base and program managers must work to establish interdependent relationships with other community service providers. Particularly as public funding decreases, programs must guard against the development of competitiveness among health care service providers that "represents the needs of the professionals instead of those of the consumer," he said. Redd also encouraged program managers to "realize the potential use of evaluation as a tool that would be used to improve program design and to influence public opinion and policy makers."

Third-Party Funding Sources

As a third-party funding source, Medicaid and Medicare should be more fully investigated and exploited, according to Robbie Littles of the Concerned Alliance for Progressive Action, Inc. in West Palm Beach, Florida. He suggested that program managers serving qualified clients should fully avail themselves of Medicaid benefits. The federal government provides matching money to those states providing coverage for alcoholism services in mental health outpatient services, in general hospitals, psychiatric hospitals, and community mental health centers and other conventional services in nonresidential settings. As options, state plans can offer coverage for outpatient services in a psychiatric facility for patients 65 or older; clinic services, including services available in (usually JCAH accredited) mental health clinics; rehabilitation services such as physical or occupational therapy and counseling offered through hospital-administered clinics; drugs; 24-hour nursing care; and home health services. (For those referral services with a high percentage of substance-abusing teenagers, states also have the option to provide coverage for psychiatric inpatient services for those under 21.)

Limited though these services may be, especially regarding alcoholism treatment services, they are still resources and worth exploring. Littles suggested that programs make sure to carefully explore client eligibility.

Private sector funding. Can the private sector replace decreased government-financed programming without jeopardizing quality, availability, and accessibility? Peter Crawford of the Alcohol, Drug Abuse, and Mental Health Administration pointed out three areas in the private (or independent) sector that are of concern to black program managers: private philanthropy (foundations, corporate gifts, voluntary nonprofit organizations, and individual donors), volunteers, and self-help organizations such as AA. The common denominators among these groups are that they are independent, usually nonprofit, and devoted to serving the general welfare.

Foundations, often described as "large bodies of money surrounded by people who want some," disburse large sums of money to selected causes, said Crawford. "Although most Americans are aware of the major foundations — Ford, Rockefeller, Carnegie — they are less aware of the thousands of other foundations, often community- or regionally-based, that together dwarf the 'name' foundations in total assets," he said. Program managers should note, however, that many of the smaller foundations "reflect the idiosyncrasies and passions of the founding donors rather than actual societal needs." Nevertheless, foundations have profoundly altered America for the better through their willingness to fund programs, research, and services on a pioneering basis, said Crawford.

Many businesses offer donations in various fashions, such as establishing foundations, presenting gifts directly to charities and institutions, and encouraging managerial and technical staff to assist nonprofit agencies. With more than $2 billion in contributions in 1979, corporations became the largest single identifiable source of giving in the nation, he said. A large number of corporations, in addition to fulfilling their economic function of supplying goods at a profit, are increasingly showing sensitivity to the effects of their operation on employees and demonstrating a willingness to serve society, even seeking out ways to do so. It may be a worthwhile exercise for program managers to examine area corporations and businesses vis-a-vis their willingness to provide funding or other support, he said. For example, some businesses may be receptive to an EAP or referral service. Other corporations may be receptive to funding or in some other way providing support for community programs.

Voluntary nonprofit organizations are another potential resource. Groups such as private colleges, the Boy Scouts, the Urban League, CARE, or any of the organizations funded by United Way fall in the category of "charitable or voluntary nonprofit organizations." One characteristic of these groups is that they raise funds and use this income for service delivery, research, or advocacy on behalf of identifiable beneficiaries.

Eighty-five percent of philanthropy in the United States comes from individual donors particularly those earning less than $20,000 per year. Leaders in philanthropy, said Crawford, believe they have an important role to play in financing health and human services programs, and rest their case on the following points:

- They have freedom from many of the constraints of public funding, in that they can move quickly to serve a relatively small constituency, are not bound by legistlation and regulations, and can afford to fail.
- They have a pluralistic approach that accommodates many points of view and approaches.
- They provide an environment for innovation and creativity.
- They provide support for ideas that have not yet gained a wide public following or acceptance.

Voluntarism is another resource not always tapped by black programs. According to Crawford, approximately 37 million Americans provided the equivalent of $34 billion in volunteered services in 1974. Volunteers serve in schools, hospitals, churches, civic organizations, and action centers and they collectively reflect "the willingness of many Americans to help others through personal action and service." Despite the changing attitudes, values and lifestyles and energy crises, inflation, and growth of litigation (especially malpractice) that has affected the willingness of some to volunteer, their ranks are still substantial and they represent a rich resource from which to draw.

Self-help organizations represent another resource in the private sector. Most self-help organizations are nonprofit-making and experientially-oriented, with many characteristics in common.

The most publicized of these is AA. It plays a significant role in meeting the needs of many alcoholism patients, said Crawford. "For example, the ADM National Data Book, January 1980, points out that of the 2.4 million persons receiving treatment for alcohol abuse during 1977, 602,000 were treated by federally-assisted programs. Of the 1.8 million treated by nonfederally assisted programs and providers, 671,000 were treated by AA," said Crawford.

No overall strategy for mobilizing resources can be complete without considering the many sources of contributions and funding available in the community, according to Ruther Carter of the Broward County, Florida, Alcohol and Drug Abuse Service Division. She suggested developing a plan for mobilizing resources to get agencies, organizations, and groups to increase human and financial assistance — funds, volunteers, equipment, facilities, office space, telephone, and utilities — they can allocate toward ameliorating community problems. In-kind contributions or pooling of material resources with other service programs is a strategy that program managers should carefully examine, she said.

FUTURE DIRECTIONS

The tone set during the workshop was clearly indicative of the attendees' perceptions of the months, perhaps years, to come: lean, hardworking, purposeful, and intense. There was a sense that professionals must be committed to more than just maintaining the status quo. Indeed, programs will have to become more effective, more efficient, and do more with less.

At the conclusion of the three-day workshop, Caldwell commended the group of participants for their "realistic appraisal" of the current situation and future directions. "We have looked at sources for program continuation other than just the public sector," he noted, "and developed a working dialogue among practitioners and researchers involved in helping blacks with alcohol problems on which we can continue to build in the future."

The sessions culminated in the identification of strategies that can be pursued to address some of the issues raised during the workshop. There was discussion of the need to expand the scope of services of many alcoholism programs in the black community to include both alcohol and drugs, as well as to develop linkages with other health services. The importance of evaluation and research in supporting program objectives was also stressed.

In mobilizing resources to ensure continuation of programming in the black community, there was an emphasis on the need for development of greater involvement in state legislative activities. In addition, there was discussion of ways black alcoholism programs can develop collaborative efforts with groups seeking to address other problems among blacks.

Working with and seeking to involve traditionally black colleges in training alcoholism researchers and practitioners was also identified as a priority by the workshop participants. Involving more blacks in research, program administration, and policymaking was seen as an important part of efforts to expand and refine alcoholism services in the black community.

REFERENCES

Davis, F. Alcoholism among American blacks. *Addiction* 3:8-16, 1974.

Harper, F., and Dawkins, M. Alcohol and blacks survey of periodical literature. *British Journal of Addiction*, 71:327-334, 1976.

King, L.M. Alcoholism: Studies regarding black Americans in: National

Institute on Alcohol Abuse and Alcoholism. *Special Population Issues* Alcohol and Health Monograph No. 4. Rockville, MD, 1982.

National Institute on Alcohol Abuse and Alcoholism. *Biomedical Consequences of Alcohol Use and Abuse and Social Implications of Alcohol Abuse.* Fourth Special Report of the U.S. Congress on Alcohol and Health (from the Secretary of Health and Human Services). Rockville, MD, 1981.

National Institute on Alcohol Abuse and Alcoholism. *Alcohol Use and Abuse Among Black Americans.* Third Special Report to the U.S. Congress on Alcohol and Health (from the Secretary of Health, Education, and Welfare). Rockville, MD, 1981.

Chapter 2

PREVENTION OF ALCOHOL-RELATED PROBLEMS: STRATEGIES AND ACTIVITIES

IN RECENT YEARS, prevention of alcohol-related problems has emerged as a key issue in the United States and internationally (Moser, 1979). Epidemiological research of the past several decades has consistently revealed a wide range of drinking problems in addition to alcoholism that have serious personal and social implications (Cahalan, et al., 1969; Cahalan, 1970; Cahalan and Room, 1974; Clark and Midanik, 1980; Rachal et al., 1980; Straus and Bacon, 1953), and the treatment system alone cannot be expected to deal with all alcohol-related problems. General public health mandates have also contributed to growing interest in prevention of alcohol-related problems placing a new emphasis on health problems associated with differing lifestyles, wellness philosopies, and possible interactions between social system factors and the health of various populations.

Recently, the Surgeon General of the United States called attention to the need for reduction in alcohol-related problems (National Academy of Sciences, 1979), pointing out that alcohol abuse plays a role in accidents, suicide, homicide, family disruption, problems in school and the work setting, and chronic diseases. Interest at

"Prevention of Alcohol-Related Problems: Strategies and Activities," *Alcohol health and Research World*, Vol. 5, No. 3 (Spring, 1981), pp. 33-41. Courtesy of National Institute on Alcohol Abuse and Alcoholism, Rockville, Maryland.

the Federal level in alcohol problem prevention programs is reflected in the Alcohol, Drug Abuse, and Mental Health Administration's (ADAMHA) sponsorship of a conference on prevention in 1979, the work of the President's Commission on Mental Health and the recent publication by ADAMHA of a draft policy for prevention program activities (Klerman, 1980).

At the international level, the World Health Organization (WHO) recently completed a 3-year study for NIAAA on preventing alcohol-related problems involving more than 80 countries and compiling information on alcohol use, alcohol-related problems, and prevention measures, policies, and programs.

Alcohol-related problems were included among the 15 most important preventable health problems in the Department of Health and Human Services prevention objectives for the year 1990. Specific goals associated with reducing the incidence and prevalence of alcohol-related problems focused on improving health status (including reductions in rates of cirrhosis mortality, accidental death and injury, and alcohol-related birth defects); reducing risk factors (including decreases in adult alcoholism, reduction of problem drinking among 12- to 17-year-olds, and stabilization of U.S. per capita consumption); increasing professional and public awareness (including increased public recognition of the relationship between patterns of consumption and fetal abnormalities as well as the relationship between excessive consumption and head and neck cancers); and improving services and protection (including increases in occupational alcoholism programming).

MAJOR RESEARCH MODELS

Approaches to the prevention of alcohol-related problems have been derived mainly from three important models: the public health model, the "distribution of consumption" model, and the sociocultural theoretical model.

Public Health Model

The public health approach to alcohol problems is of relatively recent origin, dating from the early 1960s (Plaut, 1967). Basically, the model posits three points of intervention: the host, the agent, and the environment. "Host" refers to the individual and his or her knowledge about alcohol, the attitudes that influence drinking patterns, and the drinking behavior itself. "Agent" refers to alcohol, its content, distribution, and availability. "Environment" refers to the setting or context in which drinking occurs and the community mores that influence drinkers (U.S. Department of Health, Education, and Welfare, 1978). The Prevention Division of NIAAA has been concerned primarily with projects focusing on the host, although recent research demonstration projects focusing on environmental and contextual issues have been funded.

While the public health model has stimulated considerable research and program activity, it is not without critics. Epidemiological research, a variety of ethnographic studies, and studies to determine sentiment and perceptions regarding alcohol problems have repeatedly pointed to alcohol use and abuse as social, psychological, and cultural phenomena that are beyond the purview of the public health model, or that at least complicate enormously its application to alcohol problems (Blane, 1976; Conrad and Schneider, 1980; Room, 1974, 1979*b*). Complexities in social definitions of prevention have led to the proposal of several prevention intervention models, not all of which fit neatly into the traditional public health model (Klerman, 1980). Critics question whether the health field is appropriate for or capable of preventing alcohol problems that may be more social than medical in nature (Beauchamp, 1976; Conrad and Schneider, 1980). Despite criticism, however, the public health model has provided an array of opportunities for prevention activities that public health agencies have yet to explore fully.

Distribution of Consumption Model

The distribution of consumption model suggests that a direct relationship exists between per capita consumption and the prevalence of heavy use of alcohol. Bruun and colleagues (1975) have examined this idea in some detail concluding that "changes in the overall consumption of alcoholic beverages have a bearing on the health of the people in any society."

A number of other investigators have supported the validity of the relationship between per capita consumption and prevalence of heavy use. However, Parker and Harman (1978) point out that the correlation between health damage and drinking patterns may be more significant and may be related to a variety of personal, social, demographic, and cultural factors. Makela (1978) observes that important cultural variations in the incidence of social consequences are unrelated to the average consumption level.

Certain alcohol researchers (Schmidt and Popham, 1978*b*; Beauchamp, 1976) have argued that the relationship between per capita consumption and the numbers of heavy drinkers at risk for serious medical complications is clear enough to warrant government intervention to restrict availability. However, it is far from clear what actions by government would be appropriate. A range of restrictions have been explored, though so far without substantial findings of effectiveness or a clear understanding of the attendant political and social consequences (Bruun et al., 1975; Medicine in the Public Interest, 1979).

Reviewing research on control measures, de Lint (1976) concluded that minor variations in density, location, and type of outlet; hours and days of sales; or other regulations have no measureable effect on the rates of alcohol consumption. However, rapid changes relaxing several controls seem related to significant increases in consumption rates. Popham and associates (1976), in reviewing effects of legal restraints on drinking, identified three major areas of agreement: that highly restrictive controls on accessibility lead to lower consumption levels and fewer alcohol problems; such controls are unlikely to be implemented in the absence of substantial public support; and such controls are apt to involve a variety of social and political costs that eventually will be perceived to outweight their benefits.

Considerable controversy has surrounded proposals in other nations to tighten or relax legal controls. Countries vary considerably in regulating the times that outlets may sell alcoholic beverages, and the effects of limiting the days and hours of sale of alcoholic beverages have not been adequately assessed. An Australian study of extended hours for on-premises consumption indicated no change in overall injuries in motor vehicle accidents or in the percentage of evening accidents, but the accident peak hour shifted to the hour following closing time (Raymond, 1969). In Finland, restricting retail and licensed sales to weekdays resulted in decreases in arrests for drunkenness and public distrubance (Saila, 1978).

Popham and associates (1976), reviewing the effects of controls, note two divergent opinions: that an increase in opportunities to drink results in increased drinking and drunkenness or, on the other hand, that widespread availability promotes moderate drinking. They conclude that the prevalence of drunkenness is not dependent on the number of outlets, unless there is extremely low accessibility or where a situation suddenly changes to increase accessibility (Kuusi, 1957; Makela, 1975; Amundsen, 1965).

Increasing prices has been suggested as a measure to reduce purchases and therefore consumption. The resulting reduction in demand would be expected to lead to a reduction in production. Reviews (Popham et al., 1974; Bruun et al., 1975; Osterberg, 1975) indicate that a rise in alcohol prices has generally led to a decrease in alcohol consumption, and a rise in the income of consumers has generally led to an increase in alcohol consumption. Parker and Harman (1978) suggest that income rather than price is the main determinant of demand and that heavy drinkers are likely to have inelastic demand curves. Schmidt and Popham (1978a), however, argue that heavy drinkers do have elastic demand curves, noting an inverse relationship between price and rates of cirrhosis of the liver. While supporting the contention that consumption is sensitive to price changes, Ornstein (1980) found the sensitivity to vary across beverage type. In addition, Ornstein cautioned that the effectiveness of price increases in reducing heavy drinking remains to be tested.

Few studies have focused on the effects of age limitations on drinking patterns. Increased rates of traffic accidents among young people as a result of lowering the legal drinking age limit have been reported (Schmidt and Kornaczewski, 1975; Williams et al., 1974; Douglass et al., 1974). Smart (1977) concluded that good presumptive evidence exists that lowering age limits for purchase and consumption of alcohol leads to increased alcohol consumption and alcohol problems among young people. Barsby and Marshall (1977), however, found that apparent increases in consumption of distilled spirits after reductions in minimum legal purchasing age were not statistically significant.

It is interesting to note that several of the 24 States that reduced drinking age limits in the 1970s have since raised the age. This reversal of the trend seems to have been prompted by reports of an increase in alcohol-related driving accidents and fatalities among 18- to 20-year-olds and by a continuous rise in juvenile crime.

Prevention strategies involved with reducing per capita consumption are continuing to receive research attention, and results to date indicate that the issues raised are exceedingly complex. Methods for reducing per capita consumption that are not only effective but free of undesirable long-term consequences have not yet been identified.

Sociocultural Model

The sociocultural approach to prevention emphasizes the relationship between alcohol problems and the normative patterns of alcohol use within a society (Blane 1976). Alcohol-related problems are considered likely to occur in the presence of personal ambivalence and anxiety about drinking; in situations in which juxtaposition of drinking events and social situations generates social conflict and problematic consequences (Room, 1977*a*); or in the presence of norms that encourage excessive and problem drinking. In the sociocultural approach alcohol problems may be viewed at levels ranging from the individual to the community (Cahalan and Room, 1974) to the national and international (Frankel and Whitehead, 1979). Alcohol problems may be seen as difficulties in their own right; that is, the properties of alcohol combined with the sociocultural milieu generate alcohol problems. Or alcohol problems may be seen as one set of problems in a cluster of other problems that occur in the individual's relationship to immediate and more distant social structures (Jessor and Jessor, 1980).

The relationship between the sociocultural and the distribution of consumption models remains unclear, though attempts are under way to make the two sets of theory compatible (Edwards, 1980; Frankel and Whitehead, 1979). Fresh assessments are underway to try to integrate and clarify the widely diverse theoretical and empirical data, leading to establishment of effective prevention policy (National Academy of Sciences, 1979).

The political dimension of prevention policy is reflected in the widespread debate among various public, health, and nonhealth agencies over which problems to approach and in what ways. Room (1977a, 1977b, 1979a) has explored the conceptual basis for pursuing a problem specific approach, in which major problem categories are identified based on observation and on the results of epidemiological and other research into patterns of drinking and alcohol-related problems in various groups. Six major problem areas include problems of chronic illness; acute health problems; problems of demeanor while or after drinking; casualities, injuries, death, and property loss (Aarens et al., 1977); problems of the default of major social roles; and mental or existential problems. Approaches and strategies for intervention would be based on the best knowledge available, drawn both from research and from experience, and on criteria that address the interests of the policy. Among suggested criteria for selecting intervention strategies are the severity of the problem; the extent (numbers involved or frequency of occurrence); trends in occurrence; the centrality and determinancy of alcohol's involvement in the problem; impact on others besides the drinker; effectiveness of potential prevention strategies; and ethical factors in potential prevention strategies, according to Room (1977a). This approach stresses that programming and policy be as specific as possible about what is to be prevented, and that the specificity be manageable within the context of a particular project. Such an injunction does not solve the problem of policy bias or political consequences, nor does it provide knowledge and theory where neither exists. It does, however, focus on specific and realistic activities that are possible within the purview of a given effort.

CURRENT PREVENTION PROJECTS

Alcohol prevention demonstration projects bridge the gap between the theoretical constructs discussed above and the knowledge gained through research and delivery of services. Such projects serve the dual purpose of serving individuals and communities and of evaluating prevention strategies to provide input to researchers and policymakers. The main focus of NIAAA's prevention demonstration program has been on projects that "test specific hypotheses about current and new approaches aimed at minimizing the occurrence of alcohol-related problems through means other than treatment and rehabilitation services." The specific examples that follow have been chosen because they are conceptually linked to the approaches described.

Youth

Projects for youth in educational and service organizations target the individual and rely on knowledge-attitude-behavior models of change. NIAAA-funded alcohol prevention demonstration projects directed at youth have been sponsored by primary and secondary public schools; private schools, colleges, and universities; youth organizations such as the Boys' Clubs of American and the YMCA; and treatment organizations that have youth service components. Demonstration projects at the State level have emphasized locating projects in organizations whose primary responsibilities are to work with youth. Public schools have long been popular as sites for evaluating youth-oriented prevention demonstration efforts that may include alcohol information in the curriculum, participation of target audience members in project activities, and experimentation with specialized settings for alcohol-related education and service efforts (Wittman, 1980). A $10-million program of grants to deter the use of alcoholic beverages and smoking among children and adolescents was initiated in 1980 by the Center for Disease Control. The program supports demonstrations and evaluations of community and schoolbased programs, and fosters cooperative relationships among various health and community organizations.

Two school-based NIAAA projects have tested differing approaches to curriculum development. The Education Service District (ESD) #121 in Seattle, Washington, combines alcohol information with educational theory to provide increasing increments of alcohol-related material to match cognitive and affective development. The Cambridge-Somerville Program for Alcoholism Rehabilitation (CASPAR) in Massachusetts emphasizes intensive teacher training and training of peer leaders to transmit curriculum materials. In addition to alcohol education, these programs have also developed more specialized strategies to address the needs of at-risk youth and youth who are problem drinkers.

Evaluation of these and similar projects have not been well developed for several reasons: the projects are still ongoing; the objectives of the projects were not defined in operational terms; and the effectiveness of information in causing behavior and opinion changes is not easily measured. There is a need for development of carefully designed standardized instruments and rigorous data-collection methods.

Mass Media

Prevention projects using mass media and communications organizations have included public information campaigns; public information campaigns in conjunction with community organization and outreach activities; and activities to influence the content of alcohol portrayal by various media.

Several public information campaigns using television, radio, and print media have been undertaken in the past decade. Planned national campaigns have been sponsored by the National Council on Alcoholism, the National Safety Council, the National Congress of Parents and Teachers, the National Institute on Alcohol Abuse and Alcoholism, the National Highway Traffic Safety Administration, the U.S. Jaycees, various insurance companies, private industry, and the Distilled Spirits Council of the United States. Messages have focused on acceptable and unacceptable uses of alcohol, health hazards, the problems of drunkenness, the need for moderation in drinking, and the need for action on drunk driving. The observed effectiveness of these campaigns in reducing alcohol problem behavior has thus far been disappointing, although such efforts may be effective in increasing knowledge and reinforcing established attitudes or behavior patterns (Blane and Hewitt, 1977). Other investigators have found media efforts ineffective in changing either attitudes or behavior (Cameron, 1978; Swinehart, 1972; Kinder, 1975; Wallack, 1979). However, these findings must be considered in light of the fact that evaluations of campaigns are often poorly designed or inadequate. Wallack (1980) observed that "the effects of mass media may be determined by broadening research questions so that a better overall view is gained." The effectiveness of public information campaigns as a prevention strategy may be enhanced by stress on specific problems, reinforcement of the media message through interpersonal contact, and more careful targeting of messages to specific audiences.

NIAAA at present supports public information campaigns with community outreach components. The Fetal Alcohol Syndrome (FAS) Prevention Program conducted by the California Women's Commission on Alcoholism seeks to issue warnings about the dangers of drinking during pregnancy to 1.8 million women of childbearing age in Los Angeles County, through a combination of media messages and contacts with women's groups, community groups, and health agencies. There is close coordination between community organizers and those developing the theme and content of the media material. Outcome evaluations will be based on surveys and review of birth records during the course of the project.

A second test of combining community involvement with public information efforts is underway in three counties in the San Francisco Bay area. A media-community organizing approach is used in one county, a media-only approach is used in a second county, and a control site involves no programming effort for purposes of comparision. Interim evaluations, based on household surveys, showed no change in knowledge, attitudes, and behavior in the two counties exposed to the media campaign, but some of the difficulties involved in alcohol problem prevention media campaigns have been identified. Because individual behaviors may not be affected as much as broader systems, there is a need to broaden the evaluation component.

NIAAA has also begun development of a national public education campaign aimed at women and youth. The effort will use media messages and organizational outreach strategies to supplement information provided to target audiences via the mass media with personal involvement in campaign-related project activities at national, regional, and local levels. Evaluations, designed to detect changes in attitudes and behavior are planned for each step of the campaign.

The mass media and public education project conducted by the Scientific Analysis Institute in California and funded by NIAAA focuses on encouraging mass media to portray alcohol use accurately.

Prevention intervention occurs through "cooperative consultation" with the producers of media and programming materials, based on the premise that accurate portrayals support prevention objectives and effective programming. The investigators have concentrated their efforts on entertainment programming for television, consulting on scripts and proposing programs devoted entirely to alcohol use. An advisory group of television producers has been formed to explore industrywide standards for alcohol portrayals (Wittman, 1980).

Volunteer Organizations

Efforts at the national level involving voluntary organizations in prevention demonstration projects have focused on organizations capable of reaching large numbers of people through local chapters. NIAAA has funded projects with the Boys' Clubs of America, the U.S. Jaycees, the Education Commission for the States, the YMCA, the National Council on Alcoholism, and the National Congress of Parents and Teachers to raise awareness of and disseminate information about alcoholism and alcohol problems.

Some local and State voluntary organizations have developed unique projects. The Partners Program in Denver uses volunteers called senior partners to work with youth, junior partners, who have been referred by courts and schools for treatment. The project has demonstrated an approximate 25 percent reduction in crime and truancy recidivism rates for the youth in the program and has been effective in reducing alcohol-related problems specifically. The Utah Alcoholism Foundation's "Cottage Program" in Salt Lake City had substantial success using trained volunteers to conduct neighborhood meetings to raise awareness about alcohol problems. The California Women's Commission on Alcoholism and the Wisconsin Association on Alcohol and Other Drug Abuse media programs make widespread use of volunteers to disseminate materials to local media outlets as well as to conduct followup outreach efforts. Several NIAAA-funded prevention demonstration projects receive donated time and effort from advisory groups and from other agencies and voluntary organizations.

While volunteer effort and donated time are important elements in the development of community services generally, it appears that the public at large is not inclined to organize local or mass movements around alcohol issues, despite the efforts of particular prevention projects (Room, 1977*a*). Primary alcohol prevention projects at the local level aimed at general population groups (not just dependent and at-risk groups) seem likely to face obstacles in attracting voluntary support. Two projects funded by NIAAA at the University of Denver and University of Texas are currently exploring this situation.

Replication Efforts

Part of the rationale for sponsorship of prevention demonstration projects is that successful projects can be duplicated in other sites. The NIAAA Prevention Division is completing a trial program to explore issues in replication of three prevention projects. The program tests the feasibility of transferring basic project concepts and designs to other sites. Challenges to implementation have involved accurate documentation; organizing staff, setting priorities, and working with other agencies; and creative planning to accommodate variations in site conditions (Wittman, 1980). Evaluation handbooks will be developed by original project staff (Mauss and Hopkins, 1979; White and Biron, 1979) to assist the replication site in collecting and analyzing data in a standardized format.

More recent NIAAA-funded prevention projects are conceptually tighter, more skeptical, and careful in stating objectives and intentions, more modest in who they aim to reach and what they intend to do, more deliberate in how they plan to go about it, and more careful to devise evaluations. They are oriented more toward problem solving than toward informing the public about alcohol problems, viewing information as a means rather than an end in itself. They are more likely to be conducted by public health agencies, universities, and research-related organizations than by schools, voluntary organizations, and independent service-oriented organizations. They are beginning to move beyond a focus on the individual to look at changes in minimum purchase ages, mathematical models, drinking practices and problems in communities, and institutional management and social milieu. Where the projects focus on the individual directly they are likely to use multiple and specialized techniques (Wittman, 1980). Increasing attention is needed regarding the projects' effects on the environment and the relationship of these changes to changes in individuals. To the extent that alcohol use and abuse are social phenomena, the successful project might be one that alters the regulatory, social, and physical environment, in turn creating a new set of norms for indivdual drinking practices and consequences. While the prevention demonstration project utilizing the public health model is evolving as a key tool for exploring alcohol knowledge in ways that can lead to improved prevention services, the ambitious expectation of the earlier prevention demonstration projects appears to be tempered by experience. Immediate reduction of widespread alcohol problems seems an unrealistic goal. A slow, steady pursuit of well-grounded, well-evaluated goals has received strong emphasis at the Federal level (Klerman, 1980).

ALCOHOL BEVERAGE CONTROL BOARDS

Alcohol beverage control agencies are primarily responsible for setting standards regarding the quality, availability, and price of alcoholic beverages. At the Federal level, the U.S. Bureau of Alcohol, Tobacco, and Firearms sets standards for quality and content in alcoholic beverages and establishes and collects taxes on the production of alcoholic beverages. At the State level, departments of alcohol beverage control (ABCs) or liquor control boards play a role in regulation of alcoholic beverages, including control of production, distribution, marketing, and taxation (Room and Mosher, 1979). In recent years, NIAAA has supported several research studies on the role of alcohol beverage control boards.

Another NIAAA-funded project is investigating the effect of increasing the minimum purchasing age from 18 to 21, using surveys of youths 16 to 19 years old, crash statistics, and interviews with law enforcement officers. A third project is studying the impact of changes in alcohol availability on drinking patterns and problems among university students, following a change in State law removing restrictions on off-premises sales near two university campuses. Analysis will determine the relationships between availability, drinking practices, drinking problems, and regulatory activity. Another demonstration project, sponsored by the California Alcoholic Beverage Control Department, provides training to bartenders and other servers in drinking establishments, in an effort to minimize drunk driving. The training program includes instruction in recognizing signs of inebriation, advice on how to cut off customers without antagonizing them, and steps that can be taken to promote moderation in drinking. The program has met with a positive reception by bartenders, bar owners, and the press.

RELATIONSHIPS AMONG PUBLIC AGENCIES

The effectiveness of the national prevention effort can be increased greatly through interagency cooperation, as numerous public agencies have the potential to make an impact on alcohol-related problems. Even among alcohol-specific agencies, increased cooperation is desirable. For example, there is little or no contact between alcohol beverage control boards and alcoholism prevention or treatment programs, departments of public safety, and highway safety agencies. There is a need to make communities aware of the functions and impact of beverage control boards. Local officials need information about prevailing trends in price, locations, and marketing practices in order to evaluate and assess alcohol-related decisions facing communities. Citizens also need this information in order to respond intelligently to proposed changes in zoning regulations and licensing and tax policies.

Mosher and Mottl (1980) have suggested that many agencies do not perceive the prevention of alcohol-related problems as a high priority. This suggests that prevention specialists must seek to open channels of communication, provide information and technical assistance to interested agencies, and encourage joint pilot or demonstration projects as vehicles for increasing interagency cooperation.

REFERENCE

Aarens, M.; Cameron, T.; Roizen, J.; Roizen, R.; Room, R.; Schneberk, D.; and Wingard, D. *Alcohol, Casualties and Crime.* Berkeley: University of California, Social Research Group, 1977.

Amundsen, A. *Hva Skjer Nat et Nytt Vinutsalg Apnes?* (What happens when a new wineshop is opened?). Oslo: Statens Institute for Alkoholforskning, 1965.

Barsby, S.L., and Marshall, G.L. Short-term consumption effects of a lower minimum alcohol-purchasing age. *Journal of Studies on Alcohol* 38(9):1655-1679, 1977.

Beauchamp, D.E. Public health as social justice. *Inquiry* 13:3-14, 1976.

Blane, H.T. Education and the prevention of alcoholism. In: Kissin, B., and Begleiter, H., eds. *Social Aspects of Alcoholism.* Biology of Alcoholism, Vol. 4. New York: Plenum, 1976. pp. 519-578.

Blane, H.T., and Hewitt, L.E. *Mass Media, Public Education and Alcohol: A State of the Art Review.* Rockville, MD: NIAAA, 1977.

Bruun, K.; Edwards, G.; Lumio, M.; Makela, K.; Pan, L.; Popham, R.E.; Room, R.; Schmidt, W.; Skog, O.J.; Sulkunen, P.; and Osterberg, E. *Alcohol Control Policies in Public Health Perspective.* Finnish Foundation for Alcohol Studies, Vol. 25. New Brunswick, NJ: Rutgers Center of Alcohol Studies, 1975.

Cahalan, D. *Problem Drinkers: A National Survey.* San Francisco: Jossey-Bass, 1970.

Cahalan, D., and Room, R. *Problem Drinking Among American Men.* Monograph No. 7. New Brunswick, NJ: Rutgers Center of Alcohol Studies, 1974.

Cahalan, D.; Cisin, I.H.; and Crossley, H.M. *American Drinking Practices.* Monograph No. 6. New Brunswich, NJ: Rutgers Center of Alcohol Studies, 1969.

Cameron, T. *The Impact of Drinking-Driving Countermeasures: A Review and Evaluation.* Working Paper F-81. Berkeley: University of California, Social Research Group, 1978.

Clark, W.B., and Midanik, L. "Alcohol Use and Alcohol Problems Among U.S. Adults: Results of the 1979 National Survey." Report to NIAAA, 1980.

Conrad, P., and Schneider, J.W. *Deviance and Medicalization.* St. Louis: C.V. Mosby, 1980.

de Lint, J. "Alcohol Control Policy as a Strategy for Prevention: A Critical Examination of the Evidence." Paper presented at the International Conference on Alcoholism and Drug Dependence, Liverpool, England, 1976.

Douglass, R.L.; Filkins, L.D.; and Clark, F.A. *The Effect of Lower Legal Drinking Age on Youth Crash Involvement: Final Report.* Washington, D.C.: U.S. Department of Transportation, National Highway Traffic Safety Administration, 1974.

Edwards, G. Theoretical synthesis: Discussion. In: Harford, T.C.; Parker, D.A.; and Light, L., eds. *Normative Approaches to the Prevention of Alcohol Abuse and Alcoholism.* Research Monograph No. 3 DHEW Pub. No. (ADM)79-847. Rockville, MD: NIAAA, 1980.

Frankel, B.G., and Whitehead, P.C. Sociological perspectives on drinking and damage. In: Blocker, T.S., ed. *Alcohol, Reform and Society.* Westport, CT: Greenwood Press, 1979.

Jessor, R., and Jessor, S.L. Toward a social psychological perspective on the prevention of alcohol abuse. In: Harford, T.C.; Parker, D.A.; and Light L., eds. *Normative Approaches to the Prevention of Alcohol Abuse and Alcoholism.* Research Monograph No. 3. DHEW Pub. No. (ADM)79-847. Rockville, MD: NIAAA, 1980.

Kinder, B.N. Attitudes toward alcohol and drug abuse. II. Experimental data, mass media research, and methodological considerations. *International Journal of the Addictions* 10:1035-1054, 1975.

Klerman, G. "ADAMHA Prevention Policy and Programs, 1979-1982." Prepared for the Alcohol, Drug Abuse, and Mental Health Administration, 1980.

Kuusi, P. *Alcohol Sales Experiment in Rural Finland.* Pub. No. 3. Helsinki: Finnish Foundation for Alcohol Studies, 1957.

Makela, K. Consumption level and cultural drinking patterns as determinants of alcohol problems. *Journal of Drug Issues* 5:344, 1975.

Makela, K. Level of consumption and social consequences of drinking. In: Israel, Y; Kalant, H.; Popham, R.E.; Schmidt, W.; and Smart, R., eds. *Research Advances in Alcohol and Drug Problems.* Vol. 4. New York: Plenum, 1978.

Mauss, A.L., and Hopkins, R.H. *A Manual of Evaluation Guidelines for "Here's Looking at You."* Pullman: Washington State University, 1979.

Medicine in the Public Interest, Inc. *The Effects of Alcoholic Beverage Control Laws.* Washington, D.C.: MIPI, 1979.

Moser, J., ed. *Prevention of Alcohol-Related Problems: An International Review of Preventive Measures, Policies and Programmes.* Geneva: World Health Organization, 1979.

Mosher, J.F., and Mottl, J. *A Report on Federal Regulation of Drinking Behavior and Consequences: The Role of Nonalcoholic Agencies.* Berkeley: University of California, Social Research Group, 1980.

National Academy of Sciences, Institute of Medicine. *Healthy People: The Surgeon General's Report on Health Promotion and Disease Prevention.* DHEW Pub. No. (PHS)79-55071A. Washington, D.C.: Supt. of Docs., U.S. Govt. Print. Off., 1979.

Ornstein, S.I. Control of alcohol consumption through price increases.

Journal of Studies on Alcohol 41(9):807-817, 1980.

Osterberg, E. *The Pricing of Alcoholic Beverages as an Instrument of Control Policy*. Helsinki: State Alcohol Monopoly, Social Research Institute of Alcohol Studies, 1975.

Parker, D.A., and Harman, M.S. The distribution of consumption model of prevention of alcohol problems. *Journal of Studies on Alcohol* 39:377-399, 1978.

Plaut, T.F.A., ed. *Alcohol Problems: A Report to the Nation by the Cooperative Commission on the Study of Alcoholism*. New York: Oxford University Press, 1967.

Popham, R.E.; Schmidt, W.; and de Lint, J. The prevention of alcoholism: Epidemiological studies of the effects of government control measures. In: Ewing, J.A., and Rouse, B.A., eds, *Law and Drinking Behaviour*. Chicago: Nelson-Hall, 1974.

Popham, R.A.; Schmidt,W.; and de Lint, J. The effects of legal restraints on drinking. In: Kissin, B., and Begleiter, H., eds. *Social Aspects of Alcoholism*. The Biology of Alcoholism, Vol. 4. New York: Plenum, 1976.

Rachal, J.V.; Maisto, S.A.; Guess, L.L.; and Hubbard, R.L. "Alcohol Use Among Adolescents." Report to NIAAA, 1980.

Raymond, A. Ten o'clock closing: The effect of the change in hotel bar closing time on road accidents in the metropolitan area of Victoria. *Australian Road Research* 3(10):3, 1969.

Room, R. Governing images and the prevention of alcohol problems. *Preventive Medicine* 3:11-23, 1974.

Room, R. *The Prevention of Alcohol Problems*. Berkeley: University of California, Social Research Group, 1977a.

Room, R. *Areas for development in NIAAA Prevention Programs*. Berkeley: University of California, Social Research Group, 1977b.

Room, R. *Treatment Seeking Populations and Larger Realities*: Berkeley: University of California, Social Research Group, 1979a.

Room, R. "The Case for a Problem Prevention Approach to Alcohol, Drug and Mental Problems." Paper presented at the First Annual Alcohol, Drug Abuse, and Mental Health Administration Conference on Prevention, Silver Spring, MD. 1979b.

Room, R., and Mosher, J.F. Out of the shadow of treatment: A role for regulatory agencies in the prevention of treatment. *Alcohol Health and Research World* 4:11-17, 1979.

Room, R. Conference discussion. In: Harford, T.C.; Parker, D.A.; and Light, L., eds. *Normative Approaches to the Prevention of Alcohol Abuse and Alcoholism*. Research Monograph No. 3. DHEW Pub. No. (ADM)79-

847. Rockville, MD: NIAAA, 1980.

Saila, S.L. "A Trial Closure of Alko Retail Outlets on Saturdays and Its Effect on Alcohol Consumption and Disturbances Caused by Intoxication." Paper presented at the 24th International Institute on the Prevention and Treatment of Alcoholism, Zurich, 1978.

Schmidt, W., and Kornaczewski, A. The effect of lowering the legal drinking age in Ontario on alcohol-related motor vehicle accidents. In: Israelstam, S., and Lambert, S., eds. *Alcohol, Drugs and Traffic Safety.* Proceedings of the Sixth International conference on Alcohol, Drugs and Traffic Safety (Toronto, 1974). Toronto: Addiction Research Foundation, 1975. p. 763.

Schmidt, W., and Popham, R.E. The single distribution theory of alcohol consumption: A rejoinder to the critique of Parker and Harman. *Journal of Studies on Alcohol* 39:400-419, 1978a.

Schmidt, W., and Popham, R.E. An approach to the control of alcohol consumption. In: World Health Organization. *International Collaboration: Problems and Opportunities.* Toronto: Addiction Research Foundation. 1978b.

Seeley, J.R. Program implications: Prevention. Roles in a game and way out of the game. In: Harford, T.C.; Parker, D.A.; and Light, L., eds. *Normative Approaches to the Prevention of Alcohol Abuse and Alcoholism.* Research Monograph No. 3. DHEW Pub. No. (ADM)79-847. Rockville, MD: NIAAA, 1980.

Smart, R.G. The relationship of availability of alcoholic beverages to per capita consumption and alcoholism rates. *Journal of Studies on Alcohol* 38(5):891-896, 1977b.

Straus, R., and Bacon, S.D. *Drinking in College.* New Haven: Yale University Press, 1953.

Swinehart, J.W. Coordinating the design and evaluation of campaigns. In: Swinehart, J. W., and Grimm, A.C., eds. *Public Information Programs on Alcohol and Highway Safety.* Ann Arbor: University of Michigan, Highway Safety Research Institute, 1972.

U.S. Department of Health, Education, and Welfare. *Third Special Report to the U.S. Congress on Alcohol and Health,* Noble, E.P., ed. DHEW Pub. No. (ADM)79-832. Washington, D.C.: Supt. of Docs., U.S. Govt. Print. Off., 1978.

Wallack, L.M. *The California Prevention Demonstration Program Evaluation: Description, Methods and Findings.* Sacramento: California Department of Alcohol and Drug Abuse, 1979.

Wallack, L.M. Mass media campaigns: The odds against finding behavior change. In: *Mass Communications and Drug Abuse Prevention.* NIDA

Research Monograph. Rockville, MD: National Institute on Drug Abuse, 1980.

White, R.E., and Biron, R.M. *A Manual of Evaluation Guidelines for CASPAR*. Somerville, MA: CASPAR Alcohol Education Program, 1979.

Williams, A.F.; Rich, R.F.; Zador, P.L.; and Robertson, L.S. *The Legal Minimum Drinking Age and Fatal Motor Vehicle Crashes*. Washington, D.C.: Insurance Institute for Highway Safety, 1974.

Wittman, F.D. "Current Status of Research Demonstration Projects in the Primary Prevention of Alcohol Problems." Report to NIAAA, 1980.

Chapter 3

AN ANALYSIS OF MODELS OF ALCOHOLISM AND PREVENTION AND THEIR APPLICABILITY TO AMERICAN BLACKS

JOHN S. MCNEIL, D.S.W.

INTRODUCTION

ALCOHOL PREVENTION PROGRAMS have been developed primarily from three theoretical models. They are: (1) the public health model, (2) the sociocultural model, and (3) the distribution of consumption model. In recent years, the sociocultural and the distribution of consumption models have gained greatest attention. Critiques of these models, however, have led to attempts to synthesize them and to improve upon their quality by suggesting various changes and modifications. This chapter will briefly describe these models and additionally discuss conceptual derivations of them. Their appropriateness for the study, treatment, and, more importantly, prevention of alcoholism among blacks will be discussed in the following sections.

The aim in discussing the three dominant models in the prevention of black alcoholism is to call attention to limitations that stem from the narrowness of their domains and from the lack of theory. Each model, it appears, assumes a nonproblematic relationship between the individual, drinking norms, availability, and alcohol abuse. However, the relationship between these factors must be seen as problematic and contingent upon a larger system of factors which includes other factors not emphasized by any of the models. Thus, we need a multidimensional model of black alcoholism that is capable of identifying, individual, group, community, and environmental factors and that can take account of the interactions between these factors.

DISTRIBUTION OF CONSUMPTION MODEL

Basically there are two approaches to changing behavior, one stresses voluntary motivation and the other emphasizes the use of external controls that are not contingent upon individual cooperation. These two approaches may be illustrated in an energy conservation program established to reduce electricity use. Signs are posted on the wall encouraging people to turn off lights that are not being used. Simultaneously though, management may make a decision to use bulbs of lower wattage and to cut off power at designated hours. In some alcohol prevention programs, education awareness and encouraging responsible drinking utilize the voluntary approach. The distribution of consumption model does not rely upon voluntary compliance. It argues that availability is crucial in reducing irresponsible alcohol use and as a consequence recommends the use of governmental controls. Jessor and Jessor (1980) define the distribution of consumption model as one that is focused on the level of per capita consumption of alcohol in a designated population group and the correlation between consumption level and certain aspects of problematic drinking, especially alcoholism and cirrhosis of the liver. Implications for prevention, then, are to employ a variety of governmental strategies such as pricing policies, legal drinking ages, legal drinking hours in public places, and controlling the percentage of alcohol content in beverages.

Supporters of the distribution of consumption model argue strongly that the dimensions of irresponsible drinking behavior are of such magnitude that restraint cannot be left to personal choice. Several investigators have reported studies which they believe point to a need for this approach. Parker and Harman (1980) however, in a persuasive critique of the model, suggests it is premised upon six propositions:

1. That there is a direct relationship between heavy drinking and premature death. It has been documented through clinical and nonclinical samples that heavy users of alcohol do in fact risk premature death. Mortality rates, however, vary with the method of identification of users.

2. That there is a direct relationship between heavy drinking and physical illness. Factors associated with heavy drinking such as heavy smoking, poor nutrition, and emotional distress may have an etiological role in other illnesses.

3. That the distribution of alcohol consumption is lognormal in all populations. The lognormal assumption indicates that a relatively small percentage of consumers are responsible for a large percentage of total alcohol consumption. This seems to fit, because some persons are abstainers, many are moderate drinkers, and a few are heavy consumers.

4. That there is a constant relation between per capita or mean consumption and the prevalence of heavy alcohol use. Knowledge of per capita consumption is not sufficient to predict the prevalence of heavy alcohol use.

5. That the incidence of physical health problems can be reduced by lowering per capita consumption. This proposition does not give adequate recognition to the myriad of intervening variables that may be factors in illness rates.

6. That per capita consumption can be lowered by raising the price of alcoholic beverages relative to disposable income. It has not been demonstrated that raising prices have an appreciable effect on consumption and especially upon the targeted group, the heavy drinker. Price may be elastic for the moderate drinker, but inelastic for the heavy drinker because the use value is too rewarding (Jessor & Jessor, 1980).

Of the six propositions the first three appear to be supportive of the rational for the distribution of consumption model, but the last three propositions raise serious questions as to the applicability and/ or credibility of the model. Parker & Harman (1980) conclude that "the distribution of consumption model has serious limitations. Empirical support is weak, inconclusive, and even negative both for the Ledermann proposition that there is a constant relationship between mean consumption and the dispersion of distribution for the availability proposition that mean consumption can be lowered by raising the price of alcohol relative to the disposable income. And the conceptual range of variables is overly restrictive."

In assessing the distribution of consumption model one needs to examine closely the entire availability issue and policy making relative to relying upon voluntary versus involuntary restraint. Availability of alcohol, as a means of prevention of abuse, recognizes the role of government in its physical restriction. There is a multifaceted quality to availability as pointed out by Smart (1980) when he distinquished between subjective and social availability. Subjective availability refers to the amount of energy or resources that one is willing to expend to acquire alcohol. Empirical data have demonstrated that individual's actions are influenced more by subjective estimates of costs and risks than they are by real costs and risks (Cohen, 1964). Social availability refers to small informal groups such as family, friends, and peers and the influence they exert upon one's drinking patterns. Other problems relate to the type of research that has been done which is primarily regarding availability. Most have focused upon availability and consumption effected by policy changes and procedures (Smart, 1980). Changes in availability tend to occur gradually and not dramatically therefore introducing very difficult methodological problems. When availability is related to consumption, problems arise in determining whether availability preceded or followed the consumption rate. In his review of several availability studies, Smart concluded that in some instances results were inconclusive, but in other situations governmental restriction had a significant impact. For example, there is fairly good evidence to suggest that lowering the drinking age leads to increased alcohol consumption among young people and that there is an increase in alcohol-related traffic accidents. In contrast other types of policy changes have not been as convincing. One group of researchers declared emphatically that "the availability of alcohol is an important factor in the general level of consumption" (Brunn, 1975), but another found exactly the opposite, "variations in availability had little effect on consumption" (Bacon, 1971). In a study of the 50 states and Washington, D.C., Smart found a significant correlation between consumption and availability, but an even more significant correlation between per capita consumption and income (Smart, 1980). Small changes in availability appear to have little effect. This would include such things as changing drinking hours in bars, and placing restrictions on the geographic location of package liquor sales outlets. Large changes in availability, such as prohibition, changed consumption rates but measuring illicit traffic, creates astronomical problems.

One cannot argue that methodologically and conceptually there are problems with the distribution of consumption model. At the same time, however, it does emphasize the responsibility of policy makers to consider voluntary as well as involuntary measures to control alcohol abuse.

SOCIOCULTURAL MODEL

Of the two major research models applied to the prevention of alcohol-related problems, sociocultural and distribution of consumption, the sociocultural is older. The sociocultural model focuses upon the relationship between alcohol problems and the norms in a population that govern drinking behavior. Therefore, attention is paid to the social context within which the drinking occurs. There is concern about the structure of social norms as well as the content and quality of the norms. These latter concerns, that is regarding quality and content, are the prescriptions for responsible drinking and proscriptions against excessive drinking. Frankel and Whitehead (1981) suggest that there are four sets of normative conditions that tend to be associated with specific rates of alcohol related damage.

1. Where proscriptive norms dominate and prescriptive norms are absent, the prevalence of alcohol-related damage appears to be high (proscriptive environment).
2. Where prescriptive norms dominate and proscriptive norms are absent, within the context of drinking practices that are highly integrated into the cultural structure, the prevalence of alcohol-related damage appears to be high (prescriptive environment).

3. Where the quality of social norms is ambiguous or ambivalent and drinking practices are seen as not integrated, the prevalence of alcohol-related damage appears to be high (ambivalent environment). Norms in America regarding alcohol use fall under this supposition.

4. Where clear prescriptions and proscriptions exist and drinking practices are well integrated into the culture, the prevalence of alcohol-related damage appears to be low (unambiguous environment).

From the above suppositions Blacker (1966) has altered an earlier hypothesis of Ullman and offered the following hypothesis: "In any group or society in which drinking customs, values, and sanctions — together with the attitudes of all segments of the group or society — are well established, known to and agreed upon by all, consistent with the rest of the culture, and are characterized by prescriptions for moderate drinking and proscriptions against excessive drinking, the rate of alcoholism will be low." Some empirical data provides limited support for this hypothesis, but a greater proportion of available data seriously question the hypothesis. It is believed to be sufficiently promising, however, to warrant further study and empirical testing (Frankel & Whitehead, 1981, p. 20).

Emphasis on the social and cultural components of drinking behavior highlights the fact that empirical support for this approach is sought in the work of sociologists, anthropologists, epidemiologists and other scientists whose orientation is in the social and behavioral sciences. Drinking practices would be expected to vary along ethnic, religious, or national lines. This variation would be guided by value systems, mores, beliefs, and prescriptions and proscriptions regarding drinking. Orthodox Jews and Mormons are studied as groups that have strong prohibitions against drinking. The Irish, French, and Italians are seen as groups that are accepting, even sometimes encouraging, of drinking.

Prevention as conceived by those who support the sociocultural model, would focus upon changing the quality of structure of social norms in order to decrease the prevalence of alcohol-related damage. This strategy requires the herculean task of establishing some type of national agreement regarding prescriptive and proscriptive drinking norms. In this regard, Wilkinson (1977) has suggested changes that lead to the following behaviors.

1. Drinking taking its place among other activities without special significance attached to the act of drinking itself.
2. Children are taught the customs that surround drinking behavior in a controlled and unemotional way.
3. The restrictions on the availability of alcoholic beverages are removed to eliminate the mystique that surround their use.

A somewhat similar position is taken by Morris Chafetz, first director of the National Institute on Alcohol Abuse and Alcoholism. He advocated that American attitudes toward drinking and their drinking practices be changed so that they more nearly parallel those of other countries, such as Italy, which he believed had a more healthy attitude toward drinking (Frankel & Whitehead, 1981, p. 21). A divergent stance is taken by Plaut (1972) who recommends indirect prevention methods. In contrast to the alcohol specific approach taken by others Plaut argues that alcohol prevention must be seen in a broad social context that includes other social realities. The preventive efforts must be embedded within an ecological framework. Therefore, the sociocultural model suggests numerous pathways to prevention whether they be alcohol specific or nonspecific.

SYNTHESIS OF THE SOCIOCULTURAL AND DISTRIBUTION-OF-CONSUMPTION MODELS

Considerable attention has been given to explicating the relationship between the sociocultural and the distribution-of-consumption models (*Alcohol Health and Research World*, 1981). Rather than complementing each other the two models appear to be competing. Whitehead and Harvey (1978) formulated the landmark work in the attempt to provide some synthesis for the two models. They developed a schematic of the model utilizing arrows and signs. Straight lines indicate direct effects while positive signs indicate variations and negative signs reflect inverse variation. The model recognizes the importance of the integration of drinking practices as well as prescriptions for moderate drinking and proscriptions against excessive drinking. These latter two factors are examined for the manner in which they impact per capita consumption. All then look to the effect there is upon the extent of alcohol related damage.

Whitehead - Harvey Synthesis Model

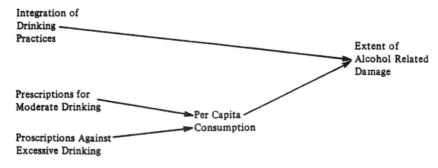

Figure 3-1.

The integration of drinking practices has an inverse variation with the extent of alcohol related damage. Similarly prescriptions for moderate drinking and proscriptions against excessive drinking has an inverse variation with per capita consumption. Per capita consumption, however, has a direct variation upon the extent of alcohol related damage. The model indicates that overall consumption is the best single predictor of the prevalence of damages.

OTHER MODELS

Among the other models are the public health and a social-psychological model that has been proposed by Jessor and Jessor (1980).

Public Health Model

Adoption of the public health model to the field of alcohol prevention was an outgrowth of its success in the area of infectious diseases initially and subsequently its extention to chronic disease. Quite naturally as public concern with socially problematic behaviors increased, strategies found effective would be applied to alcohol-related damage. The public health model uses epidemiological and/or ecological methods of investigation. Three points of intervention are posited; the host, the agent, and the environment. Host refers to the individual consumer of alcohol and his/her knowledge about the substance along with the attitudes that influence drinking patterns. The agent in this instance being alcohol and its content, distribution, and availability. Environment refers to norms and mores that govern consumption patterns and the setting or context within which it occurs. The public health model also speaks to three levels of prevention; primary, secondary, and tertiary. Primary prevention involves removing the cause of a condition before it occurs. Secondary prevention is the early diagnosis and treatment of a disorder before it is fully developed. Tertiary prevention is treatment of the condition after it has emerged as a disease before it becomes chronic or causes permanent disability. The public health model has lost some of its appeal in the alcohol field because it does not appear to offer the same success with social problems that it does with more purely medical conditions (Blane, 1976, p. 535).

Social-Psychological Model

Jessor & Jessor (1980) argue that there was a premature closure in the prevention debate when attention seemed to settle on the two models, sociocultural and distribution-of-consumption. They insist that alcohol problems cannot be understood without incorporation of problem behavior theory. One component of this is to change the opportunity structure. Limited access to opportunity, e.g., jobs, education, adequate housing, and group membership, increases the pressure to deviance, which in this instance is excessive use of alcohol. Drinking also needs to be seen within a structure of problem behaviors that exist within a larger system of behaviors. The problem drinker is therefore likely to be involved in other socially unacceptable behaviors. Thirdly, there should be some attention paid to the role of personality. Individuals may respond differently to similar stimuli. Of the models discussed in this paper the social-psychological model is the only one that emphasizes personality factors in the prevention schema. Jessor and Jessor, therefore, see their conceptualization as expanding the scope of investigation in the alcohol prevention area.

THE MODELS AND
BLACK ALCOHOLISM PREVENTION

The five models described in the above discussion suggest that they have applicability to all populations including various ethinic and racial groups. Supposedly the models are general enough and at a sufficiently high level of abstraction that they can be generalized universally. Close scrutiny, however, seems to support the idea that they were developed in a manner similar to that of most other theoretical constructs, that is patterned upon middle-class Anglo value systems. Their explanatory contribution to the understanding of black alcoholism is useful to the extent that alcohol abuse among blacks is similar to alcohol abuse among whites and/or other racial or ethnic groups. While considerable similarity may exist, the literature indicates that there are some rather distinct differences. These differences are related to multiple factors such as historical experience, sociological, psychological, ecological, sociocultural and environmental. Examination of published findings reveal many differences and Harper (1980) has sumarized the key factors in the following itemization.

1. Black females tend to have significantly higher rates of both non-drinkers and heavy drinkers as compared with white females. (61% of white women were drinkers compared to 49% of black women, 7% of white women were heavy drinkers compared to 22% for black women.)
2. Blacks have a significanlty higher incidence of alcohol-related homicide than whites.
3. Blacks on skid-row tend to drink more than other alcoholics; seem to drink most heavily on weekends; tend to be more dependent on the adjacent black community and less knowledgeable and dependent upon free social services. (Weekend heavy drinking is supposedly derived from the slavery practice of encouraging alcohol use by blacks on weekends to quell their aggression.)

4. Black drinkers attach a status element to the type of alcohol consumed. (About 30% of Scotch is purchased by blacks.) There is a tendency toward weekend drinking.
5. Treatment problems and therapeutic effectiveness differs from those of whites.
6. Black alcoholics tend to be younger than white alcoholics. (Heaviest alcohol consumption is between the ages of 18 and 34 for black males.)
7. Blacks use imaginative and creative alcohol language that is peculiar to black culture and it is often foreign to the mainstream American drinker.
8. In black communities liquor stores are often located in residential areas thereby increasing their visibility, accessibility, and frequent use. (The location almost suggests an instituationalization appearance for residents.)

The above listing by Harper is not intended to be exhaustive, but rather specification of some of the major differences between drinking patterns of blacks and whites. This listing, however, is sufficiently persuasive to suggest that the existing models of prevention, developed out of a white middle-class ideology, remain wanting when they are applied to blacks. Aspects of each of the models have some applicability for prevention, study, and treatment of alcohol abuse in black community. One would be hard put to discount, for example, that the location of liquor stores in black communities influences consumption rates. Similarly, factors such as racism and limited opportunity increase the likelihood of resorting to escapist behavior that alters the state of consciousness and dulls the pain of one's plight. Harper's (1983) listing reveals also differences in norms relative to drinking behavior. Taken individually the models do not seem to provide adequate guidance to impact significantly upon the problem of alcohol abuse in the black community.

Effective alcohol prevention is at best a formidable task and it becomes even more difficult when a program must be designed that is race specific. Several chapters in this reader describe many structured and normative features of our society that seem to increase rather than decrease the per-capita consumption rate. The schematic of Whitehead-Harvey (1974) discussed earlier in this paper attemtps to focus upon the importance of proscriptive and prescriptive norms. Jessor and Jessor (1980) do likewise in their discussion of the limited opportunity hypothesis while also indicating the need to understand personality dynamics. The sociocultural model emphasizes the need for an unamiguous environmental message regarding alcohol use. Harper (1980) speaks to the ambiguous messages that have been given historically to blacks on alcohol consumption. The black person, therefore, with an alcohol problem is "paddling upstream" when he or she seeks to get control of excessive drinking inclinations. The upstream current is beset with societal, cultural, psychological, and economic forces. A workable model must address all of these issues and to date it appears that no comprehensive model of this magnitude has been developed.

Several promising steps toward prevention have been made in spite of the lack of an adequate model. Historically blacks have tended to underutilize mental health services, but a 1976 National Institute on Alcohol and Alcohol Abuse survey indicated that black client usage of alcoholism treatment services is on the increase (NIAAA, undated). A beginning effort has been made to develop theoretical propositions and empirical facts to faciliate the treatment of black Americans who have drinking problems. It is urged that strategies such as outreach, family therapy, involvement of community leaders, and AA be utilized (Harper, 1983). Blacks have tended to overlook AA as a viable resource in the treatment of alcoholism. Caldwell, in a thought provoking treatise on AA, argues convincingly that AA has much to offer the black alcoholic and strongly encourages its use (Caldwell, 1983). Within recent years, it appears that AA groups that have been established in black settings have done well (Christmas, 1978).

A significant contribution has been made by Monroe-Scott and Miranda (1981) in the Department of Health and Human Services book entitled *A Guidebook for Planning Alcohol Prevention Programs With Black Youth*. The guidebook takes the approach that young people have the right to make their own decisions about drinking, but that they should have sufficient information to make responsible choices as opposed to dangerous or self-destructive behavior. The approach is exciting in that it includes historical and cultural material as well as data regarding ways to stimulate interest in prevention and methods of mobilizing community involvement and finally the issue of evaluation. Importantly, the young person is taught to have a positive self-image, thereby decreasing the likelihood of turning to alcohol for a psychological lift.

CONCLUSION

The prevailing models have been critically examined by several writers and they have concluded that considerable modification needs to be made before valid theoretical constructs can be developed to guide research, practice, and policy formation. These problems are magnified when the models are applied to black alcoholism.

With respect to the prevention of black alcoholism, theoretical models must be capable of delineating relationships between the host (i.e., individual and his or her knowledge about alcohol, the attitudes that influence drinking patterns and the drinking behavior itself), the agent (i.e., alcohol, its content, distribution, and availability), and the environment (i.e., the setting or context in which drinking occurs and the community mores that influence drinkers). Any prevention effort, therefore, should consider all of these factors and their interactions in developing prevention programs aimed at blacks.

REFERENCES

Bacon, S.D., "The Role of Law in Meeting Problems of Alcohol & Drug Use and Abuse," in Kiloh, L.G. & Bell, D.S. (Eds.) *29th International Congress on Alcoholism & Drug Dependence.* Sydney, Australia, Feb. 1970. Woburn, Maine: Butterworths, 1971.

Blacker, E. "Sociocultural Factors in Alcoholism", International Psychiatric Clinic 3 (No. 2), 1966.

Blane, H.T. "Education & Prevention of Alcoholism," in Kissin, B. & Begleiter, H. (Eds.) *Social Aspects of Alcoholism.* N.Y.: Plenum Press, 1976.

Brunn, K. et al, *Alcohol Control Studies in Public Health Perspective.* Helsinki, Finland: Finnish Foundation for Alcohol Studies, Vo. 25, 1975.

Caldwell, F.J. Alcohol Anonymous As a Viable Treatment Resource for Black Alcoholics", in Watts, T.D. & Wright, R. (Eds.) *Black Alcohol-*

ism: Toward a Comprehensive Understanding. Springfield, Ill.: Charles C Thomas, 1983.

Christmas, J.J. "Alcoholism Services for Minorities: Training Issues and Concerns," Alcohol Health and Research World RPO 203, Rockville, Md.: NIAAA, 1978.

Cohen, J. *Behavior in Uncertainty.* N.Y.: Basic Books, 1964.

Frankel, G. & Whitehead, P.C. *Drinking & Damage: Theoretical Advances & Implications for Prevention.* New Brunswich, N.J.: Rutgers Center of Alcohol Studies, 1981.

Harper, F.D. "Research & Treatment With Black Americans," *Alcohol Health & Research World*, Nat. Institute on Alcohol Abuse & Alcoholism, Vol. 4, No. 4, Summer, 1980.

Harper, F.D. "Alcoholism Treatment & Black Americans: A Review & Analysis," in Watts, T.D. & Wright, R. (Eds.) *Black Alcoholism: Toward A Comprehensive Understanding.* Springfield, Ill.: Charles C Thomas, 1983.

Jessor, R. & Jessor, S.L. "Toward A Social-Psychological Perspective on the Prevention of Alcohol Abuse," in Harford, T.C., Parker, D.A., & Light, L. (Eds.) *Normative Approaches to the Prevention of Alcohol Abuse & Alcoholism.* Wash., D.C.: DHEW Pub. No. (ADM) 79-1980.

Monroe-Scott, B. & Miranda, V. *A Guidebook for Planning Alcohol Prevention Programs With Black Youth.* Wash., D.C.: DHHS, 1981.

National Inst. on Alcohol Abuse & Alcoholism, *Alcohol Topics in Brief: Alcohol & Blacks*, RPS 300,. Rockville, Md.: Nat. Clearing House for Alcohol Information.

Parker, D.A. & Harman, M.S. "A Critique of the Distribution-of-Consumption Model of Prevention," in Harford, T.C., Parker, D.A. & Light, L. (Eds.) *Normative Approaches to the Prevention of Alcohol Abuse & Alcoholim.* Wash., D.C.: DHEW Pub. No. (ADM) 79-847, 1980.

Plautt, T.F. "Prevention in Alcoholism," in Golann, S.E. & Eisdorfer, C. (Eds.) *Handbook of Community Mental Health.* N.Y.: Appleton-Century-Crofts, 1972.

Smart, R.G. "Availability & the Prevention of Alcohol-Related Problems," in Harford, T.C., Parker, D.A. & Light, L. (Eds.) *Normative Approaches to the Prevention of Alcohol Abuse & Alcoholism.* Wash., D.C.: DHEW Pub. No. (ADM) 79-847, 1980.

Whitehead, P.C. & Harvey, C. "Explaining Alcoholism: An Empirical Test & Reformulation," *Journal of Health Social Behavior*, Vol. 15, 1974.

Wilkinson, R. *The Prevention of Drinking Problems: Alcohol Control and Cultural Influences.* N.Y.: Oxford Univ. Press, 1977.

Chapter 4

THE LIMITATIONS OF PREVENTION IN ADDICTION SERVICES

CREIGS BEVERLY, PH.D.

T HE INTENT of this chapter is to argue, using alcohol addiction as the foci, that prevention as a goal of intervention, noble as it is, is insufficient, and that the goal of intervention should be social development. In this context prevention is reclassified as an objective necessary to achieve in pursuit of social development as a goal. The essential question is, prevention for what or toward what end? To state the question differently, after prevention then what?

In order to pursue the argument, several dimensions must be addressed. First, it is necessary to establish the commonly understood components of prevention as a basis for definitional clarity. Second, social development has to be placed in its proper perspective in relationship to prevention. Third, theories pertaining to the etiology of alcoholism must be discussed. This is necessary because theory should guide and inform practice, and practice in turn should guide and inform theory. The relationship between theory and practice is reciprocal. And fourth, the continuum of prevention to social development must be synthesized if we are to appreciate the limitations of prevention as a goal. One word of caution is in order. The use of alcohol addiction is illustrative, not exclusive. Therefore the argument is felt to be equally applicable to other domains of human services.

PREVENTIVE INTERVENTION

Since its introduction in the public health field many years ago, prevention as a desired goal and even a preferred goal of intervention has gained increasing prominence. The work of Wilensky and Lebeaux[1] in the fifties contributed significantly to shaping thought about curative versus preventive practice with the introduction of their concepts of the residual and institutional functions of the social welfare enterprise. Lydia Rapoport in her article, "The Concept of Prevention in Social Work," elaborated on the residual and instituational functions of social welfare. She stated:

> When social work and social welfare are conceived as a residual agency, they are seen as attending to temporary and emergency problems that arise when regular and normal need-meeting social institutions break down and fail to provide adequately for basic human needs. In this residual role, social work is primarily concerned with amelioration *and direct service methods* to relieve stress and social breakdown. . . . The instituational conception views social welfare and social work services as regular, ongoing, and essential features of modern industrialized society, in which change in basic institutional patterns is rapid and ever present; welfare provisions and programs are seen as an essential component of modern life, transformed from temporary needs into basic rights.[2]

Much of the current day fervor around prevention, particularly in the social work field, had its paternity in the community mental health movement of the sixties when it became an integral part of mental health programs. Alcohol services, very often significant components of community mental health programs, began to incorporate the concept of prevention in their services portfolio. Yet, alcohol addiction service workers no less than other professionals in special population domains shared a common dilemma. This shared dilemma was poignantly discussed by Carol Meyer in an article entitled "Preventive Intervention: A Goal in Search of a Method." Meyer stated that:

> Social workers share a common dilemma with all other professional practitioners in human services. On one hand, they seek solutions to problems and are eager to track down precise

linkages between techniques that will effectively cure problems of people in their environments. On the other hand, they have a professional commitment to find ways to prevent those problems from occurring, at least to the extent that they have knowledge and skills to do so.[3]

The dilemma and corresponding debate between curative-based practice and preventive-based practice continues today. There have, however, been significant strides made in bringing clarity to the issues, particularly in understanding what preventive intervention entails and the levels at which it occurs. In effect, measurable progress has been made toward defining a method for the goal of prevention.

DEFINING PREVENTION

Too often practitioners view prevention as a unitary rather than a multi-faceted process and therefore fail to take cognizance of the fact that most writers in the field disaggregate it across three levels of focus. The three levels of focus are primary prevention, secondary prevention, and tertiary prevention.

Drawing on the work of Coolsen and Wechsler, "Community Involvement in the Prevention of Child Abuse and Neglect,"[4] and substituting alcohol addiction in their prevention paradigm for dealing with child neglect and abuse, the three levels of prevention may be defined as follows.

Primary prevention in addiction services refers to those efforts aimed at positively influencing potential abusers before addiction occurs. The key aspects of primary prevention are: (1) it is offered to all members of a population; (2) it is voluntary; (3) it attempts to influence societal forces which impact on potential abusers; and (4) it seeks to promote wellness, as well as prevention of individual and family dysfunction. Examples of primary prevention in addiction services would be national advertisements which are designed to educate the general public to the multiple hazards of alcohol use and abuse and the introduction of alcohol-related issues in educational programs of school systems.

Secondary prevention refers to those supportive services offered to individuals and families who are considered, because of their life

situation, to be at risk. While alcohol abuse or addiction may not
have taken place within these families, the probability that it will is
much greater than in the general population. The components of
secondary prevention are: (1) it is offered to a predefined group of
vulnerable families; (2) it is voluntary; (3) it is more problem-
focused than primary prevention; and (4) it seeks to prevent future
drinking problems by focusing on the particular stresses of identified
populations at risk. Examples of secondary prevention services
would be community-based efforts to limit the number of liquor
stores in an over-represented neighborhood, the elimination of pub-
licly visible street corner drinking clubs, and the availability of
community-based advice centers.

Tertiary prevention refers to the services offered to individuals
and families after alcohol abuse and addiction have occurred.
Another name for tertiary prevention is treatment. It is preventive
in nature in that it seeks to prevent future incidents or to prevent
repetition of addictive behavior by the next generation. The key elements of tertiary prevention are: (1) it is offered to persons who have
been identified as alcohol abusers; (2) it is quasi-voluntary in that often there is legal or societal coercion on abusers to seek help; and (3)
it focuses on the abusive behavior of the affected party. Examples of
tertiary prevention are treatment programs for alcohol abusers and
support groups for family members who must contend with an ad-
dicted member.

A somewhat different approach to prevention is taken by Segal
and Baumohl in their work, "Social Work Practice in Community
Mental Health."[5] The authors argue that the community mental
health movement's focus on community-based treatment and its emphasis on the impact of social life on mental status place it squarely
within the domain of social welfare. They then offer an epidemiological framework for understanding the function of mental health
centers and describe practice models that enable practitioners to
contribute to the improvement of an individual's mental status while
maintaining a view of the person in the environment and a commitment to the improvement of the overall quality of social life.

They argue further that the epidemiological framework is
founded on a preventive model that is concerned with maximum
utility of mental health services for the social group. Within the con-

Levels of Prevention Activity	Interventive Focus	Outcomes Sought
1. *Primary prevention* includes measures undertaken to obviate the development of disease in susceptible populations. It consists of *health promotion*, which includes all measures and institutions that enhance the general well-being of a population. Primary prevention also encompasses the concept of *specific protection*, which implies some knowledge of causation and consists, in the health field, of such measures as immunization, sanitation, sound nutrition, and so forth.	Mass education Public policy alternatives Alternative life styles Cultural reorientation Promotion of wellness	Eliminating or drastically reducing the incidence of addiction at the societal level
2. *Secondary prevention* generally encompasses case-finding, diagnosis, and treatment. The emphasis is on early diagnosis and treatment. While treatment specifically attends to the relief of distress as conceived in terms of secondary prevention, it seeks to shorten duration, reduce symptoms, limit sequelae, and minimize contagion.	Group and/or target (locality) specific Community organization Community education Family education Experimentation Empowerment	Reducing the at risk level of target specific and/or group specific systems-instrumental social functioning.
3. *Tertiary prevention* is largely concerned with chronic or irreversible illness; the goals are limitation of disability resulting from the illness and promotion of rehabilitation measures.	Restorative, rehabilitative Hospitalization (Detoxification) Individual counseling Family counseling Legal sanctions Behavior modification	Recreation of reasonable balance for the individual- restore to adequate level of social functioning — maintain job, family, etc.

Synthesized from Lydia Rapoport: The Concept of Prevention in Social Work

Figure 4-1. Illustrative Paradigm for Prevention Intervention in Addiction Services

text of the Segal and Baumohl model, primary prevention activities are directed toward populations at risk, that is those individuals with the highest probability of developing a specific problem but who do not as yet have it. Secondary prevention activities, such as short-term treatment and crises intervention, are associated with shortening the duration of a specific problem or treating it before it becomes severe. Coolsen and Wechler's model, previously discussed, would accommodate both of these levels under secondary and tertiary prevention respectively. Finally, Segal and Baumohl see tertiary prevention activities as ones concerned with the reduction of disorder-related problems in a population.

Though somewhat different in approach, both models discussed have implications for the main thesis of this chapter, which is that prevention has inherent limitations as a goal of intervention and should more appropriately be classified as an objective of practice leading towards social development as the goal. The argument put forth is not a devaluation of any level of prevention as herein described, for given the complexities associated with the myriad of problems of life and living there is utility and need for each type.

As will be seen later, preventive intervention at whatever level and in whatever areas is necessary for social development to take place. If strategies of preventive intervention are unsuccessful in their attempts to reduce and/or eliminate impediments to maximum capacitation, then social development as a goal of practice becomes little more than an ideal with limited to no conversion potential.

Before moving to a discussion of social development, the introduction of an illustrative paradigm would be instructive in order for one to more fully appreciate the conclusions drawn above.

A central integrative thread running throughout most interventive models is that of recreating and subsequently maintaining a balance between the person and his environment. This notion is, of course, based upon the belief that the higher the degree of disequilibrium experienced by the individual, the greater the possibility of social dysfunctioning. Correspondingly, the higher the degree of social dysfunctioning, the lower the capacity of individuals to fulfill at maximum capacity existing and changing social roles and expectations and to accomplish the various goals which they have set for themselves. The model below looks at the various levels of prevention in relation to addiction and shows the progression from tertiary to primary prevention.

SOCIAL DEVELOPMENT AS A GOAL

Professor E.P. Kibuka of Makerere University states that "social development should not be conceptualized narrowly. In particular, it should not be equated with social welfare and social care as traditionally conceived; while these are elements of social development, they are not coextensive with it."[6]

He further states that the reduction of the meaning of social development to these narrow concerns limits its scope and reduces its importance, and a development strategy which takes implicit account of such a notion of social development is not likely to result in a significant improvement in the quality of life of affected populations.[7] Indeed, the need for social work and social care often arise because of the very failure to employ appropriate social development strategies.[8] This last statement is most germane in that it effectively locates preventive strategies in relationship to the goal of social development.

This linkage can be seen clearly in the following definition of social development. Social development is concerned with the development of the society in its totality. It is a development which makes man (generic use of the term) the focus of the development effort and seeks to develop his potentialities in a total sense. More specifically, it is a form of development which aims ultimately at the maximum improvement of the material, cultural, social, and political aspects of man.

Furthermore, it embraces programs and activities which enhance the capacities of members of society to fulfill at maximum capacity existing and changing social roles and expectations and to accomplish the various goals which they have set for themselves.

Finally, social development entails in the present circumstances the democratization of the development process and the orientation of the development effort to the needs and interests of the affected population. It ensures the equitable sharing of the affected population in the benefits and burdens of development: the recovery of self-confidence and the de-alineation of man.[9]

If this definition is accepted as the fundamental outcome of interventive processes at all levels, then human services practitioners and the enterprise in which they operate must expand the boundaries of their vision and increase the scope of their responsibilities, banish myopia from their professional armaments, and unequivocally accept the notion that the ontological vocation of man is to become ever more human.[10] All activity is decided upon, implemented, and assessed in relation to its contribution on the continuum of micro to macro practice in achieving a social order where no one has to negate life in order to live.

Prevention can now be viewed as an objective leading towards the goal of social development. This is because the activities inherent in the processes which undergird it are essentially designed to minimize or remove those situations, circumstances, and conditions which force man to negate life in order to live and ones which limit his possibilities of becoming ever more human. Without the former occurring, the latter is an impossibility. The essential point to be gleaned from this understanding is very much rooted in Paulo Freire's work, *Pedagogy of the Oppressed*. In this work, Freire states that:

> While the problem of humanization has always, from an axiological point of view, been man's central problem, it now takes on the character of an inescapable concern. Concern for humanization leads at once to the recognition of dehumanization, not only as an ontological possibility but as an historical reality. And as man perceives the extent of dehumanization, he asks himself if humanization is a viable possibility. Within history, in concrete, objective contexts, both humanization and dehumanization are possibilities for man as an uncompleted being conscious of his incompletion. But while both humanization and dehumanization are real alternatives, only the first is man's vocation. This vocation is constantly negated, yet it is affirmed by that very negation. It is thwarted by injustice, exploitation, oppression, and the violence of the oppressors; it is affirmed by the yearning of the oppressed for freedom and justice, and by their struggle to recover their lost humanity.[11]

So we can see that to the extent prevention intervention promotes and facilitates man's pursuit of his ontological vocation, i.e., opting for humanization rather than dehumanization, it correspondingly makes the achievement of social development as a goal increasingly more attainable. And this is so regardless of whether intervention is focused on relieving individual pathology or focused on changing oppressive social systems.

ADDICTION SERVICES: A SYNTHESIS

It was stated at the outset that addiction services and in particular, alcohol addiction services would be the foci of the chapter but that the argument transcended this special domain. In order to bring closure to the discussion, an examination will be made of various theories associated with the etiology of alcoholism. Additionally, an attempt will be made to examine interventive methodology and locate the processes inherent therein along the continuum of prevention to social development.

In the September 20, 1984 edition of *The Atlanta Constitution*, Ron Taylor, a staff writer for the paper, wrote an article entitled, "Party May Be Over for America's Alcohol Abusers."[12] He cited all of the negative consequences and beliefs associated with causative links between excessive drinking and traffic deaths, homocides, suicides, spouse abuse, birth defects, decreased productivity, brain damage, falls, fires, drownings, ad infinitum.[13] The social cost is astronomical. In Georgia alone, a study estimated the total social cost of alcohol abuse in 1981 to be $1 billion. The study measured lost production, health and medical costs, motor vehicle accidents, violent crimes, social service responses, and fire losses. These same findings can in all probability be replicated in other states to a more or less degree, but the only conclusion which can be drawn is that alcoholism is a social problem of enormous proportions.

But some assumptions about the evils of alcohol are questioned in a definitive report issued last December by the U.S. Department of Health and Human Services. Called the "Fifth Special Report to the U.S. Congress on Alcohol and Health," it is a kind of study of studies about alcohol, analyzing reams and years of research. While many studies have tended to link alcohol abuse to homicide, suicide, rape, divorce, and child abuse, the report concludes that such studies often ignore environmental and psychological variables. As an example, the report cites suicides, saying that no study yet has proved whether alcohol causes depression that leads to suicide, or whether a depressed person bent on suicide coincidentally drinks alcohol to try to ease the depression. In the instance of child abuse, the report found some studies linking it to alcohol but others that established no correlation at all."[14]

These data, though variable and at times inconclusive, do never-theless support the conclusion that alcoholism is a social problem of enormous proportions, is extremely complex, and can reasonably be said to have multiple causation. Most authorities consider three primary sources associated with ones' proclivity to use and abuse alcohol. These are psychological, physiological, and sociological or socioeconomic causes. And even these are very often subject to the particular definition of alcoholism which is applied in the conduct of inquiry.

PHYSIOLOGICAL DIMENSIONS

Physiological theories on the etiology of alcoholism view the causes of alcoholism as stemming from within the person himself. It is essentially a genetically-influenced disorder. King (1983)[15] cites two studies in support of physiological causation. In a study of differential biological sensitivity to ethanol as a predictor of alcohol abuse and alcoholism, Zeiner and Paredes (1978) suggested possible neuro chemical bases for ethanol addiction based on differential ethanol metabolism rates. Cotton's (1977) review of the thirty-nine studies on familial incidence of alcoholism revealed that the rates of alcoholism were substantially higher in relatives of alcoholics, even when the nonalcoholics were psychiatric patients.[16]

In the August 1984 issue of the Metropolitan Atlanta Council on Alcohol and Drugs[17] newsletter, recent research conducted by Marc A. Schuckit, M.D., nationally renowned for his work in alcohol research and treatment, was discussed. Dr. Schuckit presented results of studies which he conducted on 300 healthy, drinking, nonalcoholic young men ages 21-25. One group, which had a high risk for the future development of alcoholism, had a close alcoholic relative; the control group, which had a low risk, had similar demographic characteristics but not close alcoholic relatives. The behavior of the subjects was observed after they were given a placebo or high or low dose of alcohol.

Following is a summary of his findings:

1. Data showed no difference in blood alcohol levels including: the time it takes to peak the blood alcohol level after drinking;

the magnitude of the peak of blood alcohol level; and the rate of disappearance.

2. The groups did not differ in what they expected to feel after drinking.

3. Despite identical blood levels of alcohol, those with family history positive consistently came back down toward feeling normal much faster. They never felt as drunk as the family history negative group and they developed an acute tolerance.

   Dr. Schuckit said that in a heavy drinking society like ours this presents a handicap because you don't know you are drunk until you are "very drunk."

4. In 44 pairs of subjects, the anterior pituitary hormone, prolactin, which is released when you drink, increased at the same time in both groups and then came back to normal. However, in the family positive group, the level continued to drop below normal.

5. Preliminary data on 20 pairs of subjects revealed similar differences in cortisol, another hormone which is released after drinking alcohol.

6. In seven pairs of subjects, Dr. Schuckit measured body sway, which increases when someone is drinking. The family history positives showed preliminary results of a lessor effect of sway after drinking.

7. In studying personality variables, Dr. Schuckit found minimal difference in each group after administering the Minnesota Multiphasic Personality Inventory. He found no difference between groups in levels of anxiety, extrovertism, and neuroticism.

Dr. Schuckit concludes from his studies that alcoholism is a genetically influenced disorder, supported by data from the family, twin, animal, and adoptive studies conducted by other researchers.

PSYCHOLOGICAL DIMENSIONS

Similar to proponents of physiological causation, proponents of psychological causation view alcoholism as having its basis within the person himself. Harper (1976)[18] sums up this dimension ably:

Those theorists of the psychological persuasion attempt to explain the causes of alcoholism in terms of the psychoanalysts or in terms of the learning theorists. Moreover, there are those who argue from the "personality trait" perspective suggesting that certain personality traits predispose one to alcoholism — these traits include feelings of inferiority, low tolerance level, dependency, fearfulness, low self-esteem, and feelings of aloneness. The psychoanalysts believe that alcoholism is caused by unconscious motivations (usually motivation for love, belonging, and self-respect), oral fixation (preoccupation with sucking and tasting or overly using the mouth as a source of gratification), and latent homosexuality. The psychoanalysts would take the position that alcohol for the alcoholic serves to sublimate or gratify unconscious needs and motives.

Theories	*Interventive Focus*	*Outcomes Sought*
Physiological	genetic education medical management addiction education behavior avoidance	minimize the at-risk ratio
Psychological	motivation, attitudes, values, self-esteem building, self-respect personal inventory psychic manipulation more health producing behavioral alternatives	renewed sense of potency and regaining or gaining control over one's life
Sociological/ Socio-economic	altering/changing institutional and systemic arrangements which are deemed to have a direct relationship to the incidence of alcoholism: mass education, public policy, legal sanctions, provision of health producing systems.	promotion of health through the promotion of positive support at the point people and systems meet.

Figure 4-2. Theories of Etiology and Intervention

SOCIOLOGICAL DIMENSIONS

Sociological theorists would maintain that the attitudes, values, and drinking patterns of a given culture contribute to the rate of alcoholism in that culture.[19] The author extends the sociological dimension or the socioeconomic dimension to include nonsupportive and nonlife affirming social institutions and systems which force people to negate life in order to live. Excessive consumption of alcohol thus becomes a function of compensating for impotence created by external factors (environmental and systemic). To drink excessively for all the reasons we know is actually life negating behavior, yet it is the very negation of life which provides the basis for life when the individual can find no support, no safe place, no love in a hostile world. This is particularly true for people of color.[20] Suffice it to say that the etiology of alcoholism clearly appears to be multiple in nature and though there is question as to whether all evidence is empirically validated in each dimension, it is nevertheless reasonable to conclude some degree of relatedness among and between the theories.

INTERVENTION/TREATMENT

Assuming some relationship between the theories of causation rather than viewing them as discrete entities, it is possible to develop a picture of the types of intervention appropriate at each level of causation. Even more important is the imperative viewing intervention as a wholistic process rather than a partial one. Once this has been accomplished we can return to the original thesis of this paper which argues that prevention as a goal of intervention is in and of itself limited and should therefore be redefined as an objective leading toward social development as the goal. If we can accept the concept of wholistic intervention based upon variable causation of alcoholism and the definition of social development as a form of development which aims ultimately at the maximum improvement of the material, cultural, social, and political aspects of man, we can clearly see the limits of prevention. Prevention is partial to the specific problem under consideration. Human beings must be seen as wholes and intervention must address wholes/quantum realities, which is the very basis of social development.

THE FINAL CONVERSION

The essential point for arguing that social development should be the goal of human service intervention, whether organized within the domain of addiction services or not, is that social development expands professional intervention to all levels of social, economic, political, and cultural dimensions of life.

This level of focus demands that human service professionals examine in a wholistic way all of the systems, institutions, organizations, and sociopolitical and economic arrangements with a view towards determining whether these social organizational forms operate to promote life or operate to negate life.

Systems which promote life are ones which facilitate maximum access of persons impacted by them to the fullness of their creative human potential. Thus, for example, a job training program would not train people for jobs which do not exist. Such a program would be deceiving the participant, elevating expectations which have limited to no conversion potential and basically operating on false pretenses. The inevitable result of such a programmatic response on the part of the participant would be disillusionment, frustration, and anger, forcing the person into compensatory behavior which more often than not become life negating. Such would be the case with a person in this predicament who turns to alcohol to compensate for his/her disappointment.

Social development as a focus would deeply appreciate that:

> The nature of life in our society is such that those who are unemployed are alienated from it; those who have jobs but who are unemployed, often live at the bottom of the society; and those who have little prospect of ever becoming employed live in hopelessness at the margin of despair. The job is the central status that ties one to dignity, opportunity, a human social life. The consequences of not being able to work, or of being denied the opportunity to work at the level of one's competence, is not just a matter of money loss; equally important is the consequent social status loss. Consigning people to unemployment or underemployment means consigning them to a living death, no matter what amount of public assistance we provide or for how long.[21]

This level of depth and appreciation would not permit professionals to set people up for failure. It would dictate educating participants in the political economy of the reserve army of the unemployed and it would push professionals to examine ways and means of changing the system. They could not operate on lies nor lay the problem on the intrapsychic processes of participants. This would necessitate intervention into the political and economic system through whatever means available to force humane responses to human needs.

The most important difference in social development as a goal is that it seeks permanent solutions to problems of life and living wherever institutions and systems operate to negate life and living. So while it is noble to seek to prevent alcoholism at whatever level, it is far more noble to ensure that people not only have no need to drink in excess, but also to have no need to do violence and violation to others or to destroy property or need to compensate for impotency. This outcome is virtually impossible to achieve without examining and addressing every organizational structure with which the human organization comes in contact and using every weapon in one's armament to promote humanization over dehumanization as the preferred choice for man, conscious of his incompleteness.

In conclusion, prevention is a most necessary action phase within the intervention portfolio of human service practitioners, but it must be seen as just that, a phase and not an end itself. The end product in the view of this writer is a socially developed society — one in which we strive to permanently remove from the social fabric the need for people to take revenge on life for negating itself to them.

REFERENCES

[1] H.L. Wilensky and C.N. Lebeaux, *Industrial Society and Social Welfare* (New York: Russell Sage, 1958), pp. 98-99.

[2] Lydia Rapoport, "The Concept of Prevention in Social Work," *NASW Reprints*, 1974. Reprinted from *Social Work* 6 (January 1961): 7.

[3] Carol H. Meyer, "Intervention/Prevention Intervention: A Goal in Search of a Method, Preventive Intervention in Social Work," *NASW Reprints*, 1974: 1.

[4] Peter Coolsen and Joseph Wechsler, "Community Involvement in the Prevention of Child Abuse and Neglect," appearing in *Perspectives on Child Maltreatment in the Mid 80's*, United States Department of Health and Human Services, DHHS Publication No. (OHDS) 84-30338, 1983, p. 11.

[5] Steven P. Segal and Jim Baumohl, "Social Work Practice in Community Mental Health," *Social Work*, 26 (January 1981): 16-24.

[6] E.P. Kibuka, "The Contributions of Social Science Disciplines to Socio-

Economic Development in Africa and ASWEA's Role in the Indigenization of the Concept of Social Development," Association of Social Work Educators in Africa, 4th Conference on "Social Development Training in Africa: Experiences of the 1970's and Emerging Trends of the 1980's, *ASWEA document #7*, Addis Ababa, Ethiopia, March, 1982, pp. 94-95.

[7]Ibid., p. 94

[8]Ibid., p. 94.

[9]Ibid., pp. 94-95. This particular definition was arrived at by an expert group convened under the auspices of the African Centre for Applied Research and Training in Social Development.

[10]Paulo Freire, *Pedagogy of the Oppressed* (New York: The Seabury Press, 1970), p. 27.

[11]Ibid., pp. 27-28.

[12]Ron Taylor, "Party May be Over for America's Alcohol Abusers," *The Atlanta Constitution*, 20 September 1984, sec. A, pp. 1 and 16.

[13]Ibid., p. 16A.

[14]Ibid.

[15]Lewis M. King, "Alcoholism: Studies Regarding Black Americans-1977-1980," in Thomas D. Watts and Roosevelt Wright, Jr., eds., *Black Alcoholism: Toward a Comprehensive Understanding* (Springfield, Illinois: Charles C Thomas, Publ., 1983), pp. 37-63.

[16]Ibid., p. 63

[17]"Agencies in Action," *Newsletter of the Metropolitan Atlanta Council on Alcohol and Drugs*, Vol. 12, No. 2, August, 1984, p. 2.

[18]Frederick D. Harper, "Etiology: Why Do Blacks Drink?," in Frederick D. Harper, ed., *Alcohol Abuse and Black America* (Alexandria, Virginia: Douglass Publishers, Inc., 1976), pp. 27-37.

[19]Ibid., p. 28.

[20]See Creigs Beverly, "Alcoholism and Oppression," an occasional paper of the Atlanta University School of Social Work, Atlanta, Georgia — May, 1982. Also, see Creigs Beverly, "Psychosocial Research and Its Application to Alcohol and Drug Addiction Programs," in Thomas D. Watts and Roosevelt Wright, Jr., eds., *Black Alcoholism: Toward A Comprehensive Understanding* (Springfield, Illinois: Charles C Thomas, Publisher, 1983), pp. 184-197.

[21]Mel Ravitt, "Employing the Disadvantaged," Detroit Common Council, May 10, 1968, p. 1.

Part II
TOWARD PREVENTING
BLACK ALCOHOLISM

DISCUSSION

INSTITUTIONAL RACISM and discrimination, unemployment and underemployment (black unemployment was 18% in mid 1984; unemployment among black teenagers was 43% in mid 1984), poor health and education, poverty (one of every three black Americans lived below the poverty level in 1984) (U.S. Department of Commerce, 1984), and values on the part of the dominant Anglo culture, have all had deleterious effects on many black Americans. Conjointly, these and other social forces have had significant causal influences on the rate of alcohol abuse in black communities (Harper, 1976). The dehumanizing effects of these forces must be recognized and dealt with in social policies directed at alcohol abuse among blacks. Prevention measures must be designed with an understanding of the whole set of social, economic, psychological, and political influences acting on black individuals and their communities.

Conceptual frameworks for developing alcoholism prevention strategies relevant to blacks must be based upon well articulated theories and practice models. Such strategies, if they are to be effective, must also be (1) community-based and incorporate a variety of approaches aimed at individuals at risk, the availability and distribution of alcohol, and the drinking environment, (2) compatible with existing community structures, social norms and values, and (3) capable of systematically blending current knowledge and research about the etiology of alcoholism and its prevention (Holliday, 1983; NIAAA, 1983). Unlike traditional preventive approaches which are oftentimes monolithic, insensitive, and inapplicable to blacks, innovative and promising prevention alternatives must be capable of addressing the myriad of factors and variables, and their interactions, that contribute to alcohol-related problems (Miranda, 1983; Winbush and Henderson, 1983).

With the inauguration of the National Institute on Alcohol Abuse and Alcoholism (NIAAA) in 1970, recognition of black alcoholism as a national and state concern had come of age (Gusfield, 1982; Miranda, 1983). In recent years NIAAA has given greater attention to alcoholism prevention and has established a Division of Prevention. According to Miranda (1983:162), "the primary function of the division has been the developing, testing, and evaluating of practical methods of preventing the abuse and misuse of alcoholic beverages. Some of the various other functions include development and analysis of national policy, support of model prevention projects, and technical assistance to states."

NIAAA has published an important guidebook for planning alcohol prevention programs with black youth (NIAAA, 1981). Additionally, it has published a study on services to children from alcoholic families (NIAAA, 1983). Chapter IV of this study, entitled "The Role of Cultural Issues in Service Delivery to Children of Alcoholic Familes," recognizes that alcohol problems among blacks can, in part, be explained as aspects of their general cultural, historical, and social condition. There is a new sensitivity at the federal level (and at many other governmental levels as well) concerning black alcoholism. The annual conferences and other activities of The National Black Alcoholism Council, the Minnesota Institute on Black Chemical Abuse, and other organizations have done much to sensitize people to the problem of black alcoholism. The National Institute on Drug Abuse (1981) has fostered the development of a number of publications on minorities and drugs in recent years (Austin et al., 1977; Messolonghites, 1979). While we still need to make progress on the conceptual level and on the awareness level, much has been accomplished in recent years. And now budgetary commitments must be made, research fostered, action taken.

The purpose of Part II is to provide a beginning forum for examining problems associated with alcohol abuse and alcoholism among identifiable black subpopulations. Since several recent alcoholism studies have shown that drinking behaviors are associated with gender and age characteristics (Blane and Hewitt, 1977;

Donovan and Jessor, 1978; NIAAA, 1982), it appears to us that it is important to examine these factors and take them into account in the design of alcoholism prevention strategies for the black population.

The six chapters in Part II focus their attention on crucial issues related to alcoholism and its prevention among such groups as black females, youth, and workers. In the first chapter by Shirley Wesley King, the author (1) critically examines existing literature on etiological factors in black female alcoholism, (2) analyzes and discusses major theoretical and conceptual approaches to alcoholism with a view toward assessing their utility in explaining black female alcoholism, and (3) recommends a model for alcoholism prevention measures that could effectively reduce the risk of alcoholism among this population group.

The chapter by Barbara L. Kail discusses an issue that has received little attention in research and other alcoholism literature, that is, the differences between black and white females in their drinking practices and attitudes toward alcohol. Based upon the study's findings, the author suggests that prevention measures aimed at black women who drink problematically must concentrate not only on the individual drinker but also on the agent and the environment which provides the context for drinking behaviors.

The chapter by Thomas C. Harford examines factors predictive of differential alcohol use among black and nonblack students. Using multivariate analytic procedures on data from a national probability sample of junior and senior high school students (grades 7-12), the author found that both demographic variables associated with social class and variables associated with exposure to and involvement with alcohol significantly differentiated black and nonblack drinkers. Environmental variables associated with the use of alcohol, however, did not significantly differentiate these two groups. Despite the fact that there were more similarities than differences in the predictors of alcohol use among black and nonblack students, the author suggests that future studies need to identify environmental factors which delay exposure to a more extensive network of peer drinking models and access to alcohol among black students. A major implication of this chapter is that the distinctive pattern of alcohol use among black youth is indicative of the need for broad-based and culturally sensitive programs that integrate alcohol abuse prevention measures with academic and vocational training. That is, prevention policies that result in programs for students in general may not address the specific needs of black youth.

The chapter entitled "Approaching the Problem" focuses special attention on prevention programming for black youth who have alcohol-related problems or who drink occassionally and are at risk for accidents or similar consequences. Initially it was written as part of a comprehensive how-to-reference guide developed to assist black community organizations in starting prevention programs aimed at preventing or reducing alcohol problems among black youth. It describes and explains alternative prevention approaches and examines why traditional prevention programs for nonblack youth have often not been successful for black youth; identifies nine specific prevention strategies suitable for use with black youth, including culture-specific ideas, liquor advertising surveys, and drinking practices of other cultures. The major conclusion of this chapter is that alcohol abuse prevention efforts aimed at black youth should recognize that drinking is part of black culture and, as a result, youth alcohol prevention efforts should focus on teaching responsible decision-making about alcohol use.

The chapter by Raymond S. Mayers and Carann S. Feazell focuses on the development of alcoholism treatment and prevention programs in work settings. It delineates the essential components of successful programs and points out similarities and differences in approaches with black as compared to white alcoholic workers. Major differences in approaches are related to sociocultural factors as well as the differential economic status of the majority of black workers. Major similarities in approaches are related to job classification of workers and organizational factors. The authors conclude with a series of policy and program recommendations for practitioners who work on a day-to-day basis with black alcoholics in work settings and for those contemplating the initiation of a program of treatment and prevention aimed at the black worker.

Finally, the chapter by Carolyn F. Swift and Sethard Beverly describes the development, implementation, and evaluation of two integrated pilot projects designed to test the practicality and effectiveness of providing counseling for black alcoholic offenders. The projects were implemented within the setting of a municipal court and jail and used a group of black ministers as alcohol counselors. Evaluation of the projects (e.g., Court Counselor Aides and Court Classes) indicated that they were effective in (1) reducing recidivism among alcohol offenders, (2) providing education and therapy to offenders, (3) producing a corp of community leaders with knowledge related to alcoholism, and (4) increasing treatment options for black alcoholics in the community.

In conclusion, it is critical to note that while this book is concerned with the *prevention of black alcoholism*, prevention is not offered as a rational for abandoning or dismantling current treatment approaches. We are uncertain how much time will elapse until alcohol prevention programs are a viable reality in the black community. Since there will continue to be black casualities of alcohol abuse, it would be responsible and appropriate policy to ensure the maintenance and continuation of current alcoholism treatment and rehabilitative efforts during the 1980s, and thereafter. Having said that, we must begin thinking about (and acting on) black alcoholism prevention.

REFERENCES

Austin, G.A., Johnson, B.D., Carroll, E.E., and Lettieri, D.J. (Eds.): *Drugs and Minorities*. Rockville, Maryland, National Institute on Drug Abuse, 1977. DHHS Publication No. (ADM) 78-507.

Blane, H.T., and Hewitt, L.E.: Alcohol and Youth: An analysis of the literature 1960-75. Report No. PB-268-698. Springfield, Virginia, *V.S National Technical Information Service*, 1977.

Donovan, J., and Jessor, R. Adolescent problem drinking: Psychosocial correlates in a national sample study. *Journal of Studies on Alcohol, 39*, 1506-1524, 1978.

Gusfield, J.R.: Prevention: Rise, decline and renaissance. In Gomberg, E.L., White, H.R., and Carpenter, J.A. (Eds.): *Alcohol, Science and Society Revisited*. Ann Arbor, Michigan, The University of Michigan Press, 1983, pp. 402-425.

Harper, F.D.: *Alcohol Abuse and Black America*. Alexandria, Virginia, Douglass Publishers, 1976.

Holliday, B.G.: Making the best of a bad situation: Pragmatic planning strategies for black alcohol prevention efforts in the 1980s. In Watts,

T.D., and Wright, Jr., R. (Eds.): *Black Alcoholism: Toward a Comprehensive Understanding.* Springfield, Illinois, Charles C Thomas, Publisher, 1983, pp. 152-161.

Messolonghites, L.A.: *Multicultural Perspectives on Drug Abuse and Its Prevention: A Resource Book.* Rockville, Maryland, National Institute on Drug Abuse, 1979. DHHS Publication No. (ADM) 78-671.

Miranda, V.L.: Black alcohol prevention programming, past, present, future. In Watts, T.D., and Wright, R. Jr., (Eds.): *Black Alcoholism: Towards a Comprehensive Understanding.* Springfield, Illinois, Charles C Thomas, Publisher, 1983, pp. 162-173.

National Institute on Alcohol Abuse and Alcoholism. *A Guidebook for Planning Alcohol Prevention Programs with Black Youth.* Rockville, Maryland, 1981.

National Institute on Alcohol Abuse and Alcoholism. *A Growing Concern: How to Provide Services for Children from Alcoholic Families.* Rockville, Maryland, 1983. DHHS Publication No. (ADM) 83-1257.

National Institute on Drug Abuse. *A Guide to Multicultural Drug Abuse Prevention.* Rockville, Maryland, 1981.

U.S. Department of Commerce. *Money Income and Poverty Status of Families and Persons in the United States: 1984.* Washington, D.C., U.S. Bureau of the Census Series P-60, No. 136-140, Issued Jan.-July, 1984.

Winbush, R.A., and Henderson, P.S.: We may as well try this: Some reflections on alcohlism services research in the African-American community. In Watts, T.D., and Wright, R., Jr. (Eds.): *Black Alcoholism: Toward a Comprehensive Understanding.* Springfield, Illinois, Charles C Thomas, Publisher, 1983, pp. 198-205.

Chapter 5

BLACK FEMALES AND ALCOHOLISM PREVENTION STRATEGIES

SHIRLEY WESLEY KING, PH.D.

INTRODUCTION

A LCOHOLISM in the United States is a problem of monu-
mental proportions. Its effects extend beyond those who are alcoholics themselves to include those significant others who have
concern about their well-being as well as others outside of the family
network. For example, hospital reports of patients of automobile accidents and homicides attest the magnitude of this problem.

Within the black community, the impact of alcoholism is so destructive that it is second only to the deadly disease of racism as a
health and social problem. In this regard, Bourne (1973:211) has
stated that alcoholism ranks almost certainly as the number one
mental health problem, if not the most significant health problem.
One expert on alcohol and blacks declares alcohol to be *the* number
one social problem in black America (Harper, 1976:1).

Much of the research work has centered around efforts to establish prevalence rates of alcoholism among blacks. Perhaps of greater
concern is the fact that research in this area has not emerged beyond
attempts to establish prevalence rates on a comparative basis. This
narrow approach has inhibited our ability to fully understand the
black experience with alcohol abuse/alcoholism. Operating in this

manner will not enable us to determine factors that distinguish blacks as victims of this disease. Many key questions have not yet been answered. For example, questions remain about the role culture plays in the drinking practices of groups of people, and to what extent social norms serve to shape or control drinking patterns.

In the few and rare situations where blacks have been examined, the study samples have focused primarily on black men. The literature reflects a paucity of empirical research which illucidates the experiences of black females with alcohol abuse and alcoholism. Thus, what can be gleaned about alcohol abuse and alcoholism among black females must be abstracted from the available literature on blacks (ala black men) and women (ala white females). Neither group serves as an adequate or sufficient norm by which to gauge the experiences of black females.

This chapter is an attempt to better understand black female alcohol abuse and alcoholism by: (1) examining the available literature on blacks and alcoholism, and women and alcoholism, (2) discussing the implications and explanatory nature of this literature as it relates to black females and alcohol abuse and alcoholism, and (3) recommending some prevention strategies to minimize the incidence of alcoholism among this highly at-risk subgroup.

ALCOHOL USE AND ALCOHOLISM
AMONG BLACK AMERICANS

In general, there is consensus that blacks begin drinking at an earlier age than whites (Viamontes and Powell, 1974); blacks begin drinking heavily at an earlier age than whites (Robins and Guze, 1971; Viamontes and Powell, 1974); and blacks experience more alcoholism-related problems than whites (NIAAA, 1981). While these patterns appear to be fairly well documented, there is less understanding and documentation of the etiology of this problem among blacks. Some research studies have provided more insight into the drinking practices and impact of alcohol abuse on the health status of blacks. Unfortunately, what is known about the general health status of blacks is not very positive. Findings reported by Haynes (1975) illustrate this point. His results show that black adults are twice as likely as whites to have heart disease, black men are three times more likely than white men to have hypertensive heart disease, and blacks have higher rates of cancer than whites. Moreover, black men and women surpass their white counterparts in rates of cancer of the prostate and cancer of the cervix, respectively (Leffall, 1975). There is additional evidence that blacks also exceed whites in rates of the disease alcoholism and in rates of physiological illness resulting from alcohol abuse. A study by Rimmer et al. (1971) of white and black alcohol patients from two midwestern hospitals, indicates that more blacks (52%) than whites (11%) reported hospital admission for medical complications associated with alcoholism and, that more blacks than whites had cases of delirium tremens (54% versus 25%) and alcoholic hallucinosis (47% versus 16%). The only exception to this pattern was reported in the finding that in this same sample, whites revealed more evidence of liver damage than blacks (20%) versus (6%). Furthermore, black women experienced more hospitalizations than both black and white men and white women, and were more likely to go on a "bender" than were white women.

The results reported by Rimmer et al. (1971) contradict findings cited earlier by Kuller et al. (1966). The findings by Kuller et al. (1966) indicated that young blacks of a mideastern city suffered more liver damage from alcoholism than did whites and that more black men (25%) and black women (39%) than white men (19%) and white women (38%) died from liver disease.

In an attempt to assess alcoholism as a public health problem, Bailey et al. (1965) used a sample of 4387 black and white families from New York City. Results from their epidemiological study indicated that the rates of alcoholism for blacks from families of low income, poor housing, and high occupational and residential mobility were among the highest. Additionally, black urban alcoholics presented more chronic physical illnesses and health problems than did the general adult population. The black alcoholics also presented greater evidence of emotional strain and psychological impairment.

Corroborating findings were reported by Rosenblatt et al. (1971) which indicated that community health factors were associated with alcoholic family members. Their work revealed that problem drinking among their sample was characterized by overcrowded housing, veneral disease, juvenile delinquency, tuberculosis, unemployment, low educational levels, and high rates of aid to dependent children. These researchers also reported that black alcoholics from such high density and problem-proned communities were susceptible to "alcoholic psychoses" and early psychological breakdown. The researchers concluded that social and demographic factors of urban low-income communities are related to a high incidence of alcohol withdrawal syndromes.

Summarily, these findings suggest that blacks are indeed victims of a number of forces which combine to make them more likely abusers of alcohol and/or candidates of the disease alcoholism. Although strong empirical evidence is lacking, these findings also suggest that one's health status, which is related to socioeconomic status, heavily influences the impact alcohol has on the physiological condition. Consequently, the socioenvironmental forces combined with the drinking practices of blacks may account for a higher incidence of alcohol abuse and alcoholism. Drinking behavior for black men tends to also be linked with factors that are "ego gratifying" in nature. The precipitating and nurturing elements for their drinking behavior appears to be intimately tied to social norms which perceive such drinking behavior as acceptable and even expected. Because there is little empirical research available which has used blacks as study samples, much of the information about blacks and alcohol use is merely speculative. Efforts have been made, however, to delineate factors that are believed to significantly contribute to the drinking practices and patterns among blacks. In this regard, the following random observations have been noted:

(1) The black community is less apt to view alcoholism as an illness than the white group. There is greater denial of the condition among blacks.

(2) The black community exhibits a greater tolerance of the alcohol abuser.

(3) Escape drinking and depression appear to be more prominent among black teenage alcohol abusers.

(4) Distinctive problems of alcohol abuse among blacks are largely the result of more heavily weighted tensions and frustrations visited upon blacks through racial barriers which inhibit full participation in American society.

(5) Drinking practices as a "rite of passage" for many young black males is a sign of manhood. This practice is akin to the reports consistently made by behavioral scientists that there is a compulsive human need to emulate one's version of a "success model."

(6) The socioeconomically-deprived have a lower threshold for self and other definitions of alcoholic abuse as a problem. In contrast, the more advantaged blacks are extremely reluctant to become visible as problem drinkers to the point of not seeking necessary assistance from public agencies.

(7) There is a higher incidence of alcohol abuse and alcoholism in the products of broken homes. Since there are a greater number of one-parent homes among blacks, there is a correspondingly higher incidence of alcoholism among blacks of broken homes.

(8) The black alcoholic tends to seek treatment at a much later phase in his illness. It has been surmised that this practice is encouraged by the higher tolerance of drinking behavior.

(9) Presumptive evidence indicates that there are proportionately larger numbers of blacks who are problem drinkers and alcohol abusers in America. In spite of this evidence, virtually nothing is known about the nature of this problem among blacks, especially for those not found on skid row. (McAlpine, 1973).

Certainly these observations will add much to future investigations into this problem area by serving as the basis for hypotheses to be tested. However, the void of information relative to black females and alcohol use remains. Since men and women are socialized differently, it should be expected that drinking behaviors and practices among females will be motivated, in part, by some factors that are unique in that regard. Thus, prevention and treatment must be guided by what we know about females who are black and alcohol abusers.

ALCOHOL USE AND ALCOHOLISM
AMONG FEMALES

Because so little research has been conducted on the female alcoholic, what can be definitively stated about them is extremely limited. A major distinction about the female alcoholic in comparison to the male alcoholic is that alcoholism within this group tends to be more individual. For example, there may be more variability among women alcoholics in the circumstances surrounding the onset of excessive drinking. That is, the immediate precipitating causes of the alcoholism may be more variable for women than for men alcoholics. There may also be more variability among women alcoholics in maintaining their alcoholism. It may be that women alcoholics continue their problem drinking past the point of its beginning for more variable reasons than do men alcoholics.

While few validated answers to the above assertions exist, there is a clearer picture with respect to precipitating factors of female drinking behavior. For example, Wall (1937) has stated that among women alcoholics, ". . . the excessive drinking (is) more intimately associated with a definite life situation." An interpretation of this finding is that among women, alcoholism is more likely to be associated with some concrete situation than is true among men.

Research works which seek to empirically document drinking practices and patterns of female alcoholics provide additional though limited insights on this issue. Knupfer (1963) makes a connection between social pressure and unrestrained drinking by women as a means of abetting their sexual restraints, and the ability of men to gain compliance with these behavioral standards by virtue of the economic dependence of women. Thus, in groups where women are less economically dependent on men, their behavior should more closely resemble that of men. The author suggests that the risk for the development of alcoholism may be proportionately larger among Negro than white females.

Several studies have noted that gender is an important variable in drinking behavior among blacks and between blacks and whites. The literature strongly indicates that race and gender differences are important explanatory variables when trying to understand alcohol abuse. Research by Cahalan, Cisin, and Crossley (1969) found that black men and white men in their national probability sample did not differ significantly from each other in terms of rates of drinking. Yet the situation was quite different for black females in comparison to white females. While there were fewer drinkers among the sample of females (49% for blacks and 61% for white females), black females made up a greater proportion of those labeled heavy drinkers (i.e., the percentages were 22 and 7 for black women and white women, respectively). These authors concluded that fewer black females drink, but when they do, they were more likely, compared to white females, to be heavy drinkers.

In an earlier study of black-white differences in heavy drinking, Sterne (1967) indicated that rates of alcoholism among black females were uniformly higher than those for white females. Thus, the author hypothesized that black females run a much higher risk of becoming heavy drinkers than do their white counterparts.

Findings by Locke et al. (1960) revealed that even when education is controlled, urban black female rates were higher than for whites at each level of education (from three to six times higher). This discrepancy between black and white females rose with increasing educational attainment. Controlling for employment status, adjusted rates of alcoholism among employed black females were over three times higher than those employed white females; for black female homemakers, the rate was 5.5 times higher than that of white females who were also homemakers.

The more recent research findings raise questions about the previously reported black-white female differences in rates of heavy drinking. Therefore, it is appropriate that the earlier reports on this topic be interpreted with caution. Just as it would be faulty to generalize drinking practices of other groups using the norm established on white males, similarly it is inappropriate to generalize to all females the norms established on white females.

A composite of available information on drinking patterns among women suggests a "profile" which indicates that:

> On the average, women were older at their first drink, tended to drink alone, tended to drink distilled spirits, were periodic or binge drinkers, and tended to move more rapidly into alcoholism (Lowenfish, 1977). Furthermore, they tended to also belong to religious groups with proscriptions against alcohol, but those women who were church-goers were less likely to drink. A significant number of women had mothers who drank, although if the father was an abstainer, the daughter was more likely to abstain also (Keil, 1978). Over 50 percent of the women drinkers were divorced or had never married (Weschler et al, 1978). Women

with the lowest education were the highest abstainers (Klatsky et al, 1977a), while the inverse was true for men. Research findings by Sieber (1979) indicated that women with the lowest social integration tend toward heavy drinking.

Again, evidence would suggest that sociocultural practices and socialization appear to be associated with drinking practices of females. While black females share some of the experiences of white women as dictated by socialization practices governed through sociocultural norms, because of their unique racial and cultural heritage, black females' drinking practices may be different as they will be shaped by these distinctions. The literature is grossly lacking in sufficiently addressing concerns raised about black females and alcohol abuse and alcoholism.

ALCOHOLISM AND THE BLACK FEMALE

The most recent review of the literature on alcohol and black Americans reveals that there are no articles that focus primarily on alcoholism and black women (Harper, 1983). Gaines (1976) is cited as the sole source for theoretical insights and other related information on the problem. The work written by Gaines entitled "Alcohol and the Black Woman" cites these observations: (1) black women tend to have higher rates of abstainers and heavy drinkers when compared with white women (Cahalan and Cisin, 1968), (2) black women indicate stronger interest in treatment than black men and the rate of treatment success for black women is higher (Strayer, 1961), and (3) black female heavy drinkers in a city are likely to be household heads, generally impoverished and to have drinking styles and behaviors similar to those of black male heavy drinkers (Sterne and Pittman, 1972). While these observations are helpful in trying to understand black females and alcohol use and/or abuse, many questions remain unanswered. Other works which have implications for black female alcoholism, present findings of a comparative nature between black and white females and blacks and whites in general (Cahalan et al, 1969).

These sketchy findings do little more than point out how much we do not know about black female alcohol abuse and alcoholism.

For example, we need to be able to answer questions about whether the female role is changing or not? And if so, to what extent (if any) will it affect black women? What are the implications of these changes for their drinking practices?

The state of knowledge on this subject is so underdeveloped that to talk about "the black female alcoholic" is preposterous. Such labelling suggests that sufficient empirically established facts, are known about the character and nature of this population. However, quite the contrary is true. Currently, the literature only substantiates that there are black females who abuse alcohol and are victims of alcoholism (heavy drinking). The little research that does exist is wrought with methodological frailties which has caused the image of black female alcoholics to be skewed. Most studies have used samples of institutionalized populations (i.e., correctional facilities or hospitals) because they are captive audiences. Thus the profile characteristics are not generalizable to the general black female alcoholism population. Since individuals of the lower socioeconomic strata are more likely to be products of these institutions, certain characterisitics of this group have erroneously been used to establish a norm for black female alcoholics. For example, black females of the lower socioeconomic strata are more likely to be single, heads of households, and possibly part of a sociocultural environment which tolerates drinking behavior, which also makes them more likely to be a greater risk to alcoholism. Furthermore, evidence indicates that drinking is highest among divorcees under forty-five years old; that the lower socioeconomic strata has the lowest proportion of drinkers or abstainers. Although these characteristics may represent one model of the black female drinking population, they do not necessarily reflect the full range of characteristics that exist among black female alcohol abusers or alcoholics. The case that follows is illustrative of the variation in characteristics that can be found among black female alcoholics.

> Linda X, a 24-year-old high school graduate and national merit scholar, started drinking when she was seventeen. Her drinking began as a social activity which masked her shyness and enabled her to interact with others more easily. It was not until Linda X was a college freshman that she began to realize that her drinking extended beyond her social encounters, to drinking alone. Al-

though she recognized that her drinking was a problem at that time, she did not accept that she was an alcoholic. Instead, she continued to drink and experience the troubles commonly associated with meeting drinking needs with limited resources. After losing her four-year scholarship, Linda saw herself as a failure and drank more to forget her sorrows. Having dropped out of several treatment programs, Linda did not really begin to take control of her drinking problem until she acknowledged that she was an alcoholic. Linda X is now involved in a residential treatment program which is geared specifically for women and uses a mutual aid support system to help women help each other in combatting this problem. Linda X states that one of the most significant factors for her adhering to this program is the fact that it is run by people who are experienced in the problem as well as in treatment approaches. Linda states that "because the director is a recovering alcoholic and a black female, I can't lie to them or myself anymore."

There are clearly significant aspects of this case profile that have implications for the study and understanding of black female alcoholics. Future research must surely develop study designs that will assure sample representativeness of black alcoholics which will enable a realistic appraisal of the role such variables as gender, socioeconomic status, family relationships, etc., play in the development and maintenance of alcohol abuse and alcoholism. Moreover, until this level of understanding is developed, treatment and prevention strategies will continue to be hampered.

That alcohol abuse and alcoholism are grave social problems for blacks, and black females in particular, is a fact. The multifaceted nature of the problem (causes, facilitators, and manifestations) belies any attempts of simplistic solutions. Efforts to devise effective treatment and prevention strategies will have to include: (1) a Black Cultural Approach, (2) a Community-wide Approach, and (3) a Gender Sensitive Approach.

PREVENTION STRATEGIES
AND THE BLACK FEMALE

Prior to the 1970s most initiatives to combat alcoholism were anchored in a variety of treatment modalities. The seventies and eighties are now directing a great deal of attention to prevention approaches. Although much controversy is centered around the concept, there remains much expectation about the potential impact such a practice can conceivably attain. The salient questions with respect to alcohol prevention strategies for black females are: (1) how can prevention approaches be used to reduce the incidence of alcoholism among black females at high risk? and (2) in what ways can the central systems which most heavily influence black females be tapped towards that end?

The three essential prevention aspects to be addressed in this very complex problem are quite similar to the three classic intervention levels of the public health model. The public health model was created by the Cooperative Commission on the Study of Alcoholism (Plaut, 1967). The model basically involves three points of intervention: (1) the *host* (the individual and his/her knowledge about alcohol, the attitudes that influence drinking patterns, and the drinking behavior itself), (2) the *agent* (alcohol, its content, distribution, and availability), and (3) the *environment* (the setting or context in which drinking occurs and the community mores that influence drinkers (USDHEW, 1978).

Most of the work conducted by the Prevention Division of the National Institute of Alcohol Abuse and Alcoholism has focused on the first component giving little to no attention to the agent and/or environment. Failure to undertake a holistic approach to this massive problem has resulted in the continued growth of this devastating disease. More recent investigations have recognized the importance of the role the agent and environment may play in alcohol prevention strategies. For example, King (1979) states that perhaps the key to prevention strategies is the extent to which a community has defined and legitimized, within its folkways and mores, alcoholism as a problem. Another writer has surmised that it is important to know what the attributes are of the community and family concerning the problem and its cause (McKirnan, 1978). Moreover, the question has been asked, to what extent does a person's violation of the norms of the group lead to some early or primary identification of that person as having a problem?

Of the extremely few efforts devoted to black alcohol prevention, Miranda (1983) has devised what might be the foundation for a comprehensive, strategic, pragmatic course of action towards effectively addressing the black alcohol problem. The idea outlined by Miranda is premised on the notion that "alcohol abuse prevention for black communities is inherently different from prevention for white communities. The differences derive primarily from a difference in needs and the singular nature of black history" (NIAAA, Black Panel of Experts, 1979).

For the purposes of this chapter, I have used a modified version of the Miranda model in developing an approach to alcohol prevention strategies for black females (see Fig. 5-1). An essential aspect of the Miranda approach was based on results of surveys conducted in three Black communities which yielded four variables as major influences in youthful drinking; value system, role models, media, and the environment including unemployment and easy access to liquor. *Value system* was conceived as that set of influences which sanctions behavior through approval/disapproval or ignored standards. Black females (youths) may accept, reject, add to or subtract from these standards. The extent to and manner in which they do so will largely depend on whether the black community and larger community provide positive value systems which enable them to build self-pride as a member of a distinct cultural group. Much attention has been devoted to the issue of black self-pride/self-concept in light of racial discrimination (Poussaint and Atkinson, 1972). The challenge to the black family and black community is indeed, the extent to which they can transcend the negative forces of racism and meet the extraordinary function of providing positive, nurturing experiences which form the basis of self-esteem. The family is the first place in which one gains a sense of who he/she is and what one can and ought to become (Clarke, 1978). The black community as well as the larger society must ask the question: What are the messages given black females regarding drinking practices? What are the value sets that serve as guiding principles for black females? The answers to these questions must shape the response(s) developed to counter alcohol abuse and alcoholism.

The second area, *role models*, provides images to emulate as youth make their transition into adulthood (Donovan and Jessor, 1978). Many studies have documented that children pattern the alcohol be-

havior seen most often. The literature indicates that female alcoholics tend to emerge from settings where their mothers were heavy
drinkers, and to be abstainers more often where the fathers were abstainers. Because alcohol research samples have not been randomly
drawn from the general black (female) population, it is not known to
what extent and in what way black females at all socioeconomic
strata are affected by alcohol abuse and alcoholism. However, when
applying the above information to those black female subjects who
have been studied, it is reasonable to expect that a cycle is in motion.
Modeling behavior is in force for the black female who is the product
of a broken home where the father is likely to be absent and the
mother is head of the household and perhaps is a heavy drinker.
That female is probably a good candidate for the statistic of black female alcoholic. Other influential models come from the street,
church, media, as well as a host of other sources.

The *media*, the third area, has been cited as the number one
culprit in presenting alcohol use in a positive, glamorous way and as
representing maturity and sophistication. In the black community
the model is presented as an attractive black female who exudes an
air of success. Such images are most difficult to combat. Finally,
there is the influence of the environment such as unemployment
rates and high accessibility to liquor stores (Dawkins, 1983), and the
high visibility of the corner drunk seen every day by school children.
All of these elements reinforce a negative self-image at the individual
as well as community level.

What can feasibly be done to counter these destructive influences
on black females? The black community has a wealth of resources in
the form of organizations. Many of these organizations have identified improving self-image or self-pride as one of their major goals.
The primary prevention approach suggested in this paper flows out
of the recognition that black females, more so than black males, are
a part of a complex socializing network. This network includes family (immediate and extended), school, church, and community.
However, an all out collective, deliberate attack must be directed at
this problem. Consequently, every black organization (professional,
civic, and service) must identify and adopt a specific role in combatting this problem.

It is the position of this writer that the black community's major problem in this area rests in a lack of sensitivity to the seriousness of the problem. The fact that evidence indicates a higher tolerance of alcohol behavior is reflective of this lack of understanding. Black health and mental health professionals must take the leadership in helping other organizations to understand the problem and define appropriate roles for them to serve as intervention specialists. Research has documented that cultural factors play a significant role in whether, how much, and why a person drinks. Even without available research which empirically delineates how culture among blacks influences drinking practices and patterns, the prevalence data already indicate a dire need to reverse the effects on blacks. This is even more critical for black females since they are at a higher risk than any other subgroup studied.

It is the black community's challenge to develop linkages among the vast array of organizations mentioned above for the expressed purpose of education and reeducation towards responsible drinking. Furthermore, the black community and only the black community, vis-a-vis the family and other community systems, can foster a black values system which is strong enough to offset any would-be debilitating forces to the black community — alcohol abuse is no exception. Externally, the black community must develop linkages with the National Institute on Alcohol Abuse and Alcoholism to attack this problem. This suggestion is based on the recognition, first that black American females reside in dual societies — an African-American society and a larger society, dominated by Anglos, but inclusive of other racial and cultural groups. This duality calls our attention to the fact that responses to the needs of black people in general, must combine efforts from both spheres.

Miranda outlines the following steps as a method of developing black alcohol prevention strategies:

(1) National Black Alcoholism Council (NBAC) should develop a policy statement that would demand NIAAA to respond to the black alcohol prevention needs in the United States, and NBAC should appoint a prevention committee to monitor NIAAA's efforts.

(2) NIAAA should fund priorities directed at prevention programming for blacks and work statements delivered to its branches and NIAAA's National Clearinghouse for Alcohol Information (NCALI).

(3) The clearinghouse should stimulate and assist community-based organizations in developing programs for black youth through working relationships with black churches.

(4) National black church affiliations (i.e., national Baptist convention, black Catholic clergy, etc.) should proclaim black alcohol problem prevention a major concern of the black church and black community and sponsor programmed activities to respond to the proclamation.

(5) Community social change efforts initiated by the church in response to the need of self-solution (Miranda, 1983).

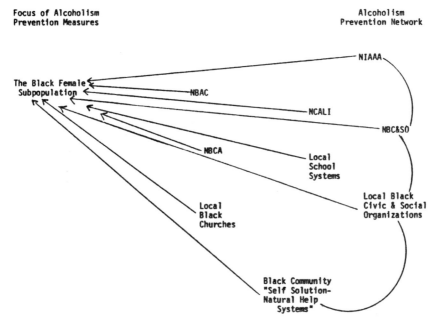

Focus of Alcoholism
Prevention Measures

Alcoholism
Prevention Network

The Black Female Subpopulation

NIAAA

NBAC

NCALI

NBC&SO

NBCA

Local School Systems

Local Black Churches

Local Black Civic & Social Organizations

Black Community "Self Solution-Natural Help Systems"

Figure 5-1. Essential Components of An Integrated Approach to Black Female Alcoholism Prevention

While, I subscribe, in principle, to the philosophy, orientation, and direction outlined in the seminal work by Miranda, I believe that a holistic approach to the prevention of black female alcoholism must encompass all the resources in the black community and society that could impact upon black females at-risk of alcoholism. Figure 1 presents an integrated framework for black female alcoholism prevention.

This framework provides a summary of the ideas discussed so far and suggests that prevention may be viewed as a process which involves elements from all levels of society (i.e., natural helping systems, the school system, national and local black civic and social organizations, federal and national organizations concerned with alcoholism, etc.). The integration and coordination of these multiple prevention forces is deemed necessary to effectively ameliorate and prevent alcoholism among black females.

Unlike Miranda's schema, the integrated framework shows that there are many points in the social system in which prevention actions can be initiated and implemented. Regardless, however, where action is initiated, it is important that these efforts be coordinated and synthesized with the efforts of other system components. This will ensure the best possible use of scare resources and that prevention efforts are effective and efficient in mitigating the problem within the target population.

An integrated alcoholism prevention approach can go a long way in reducing the prevalence and incidence of alcoholism not only in the target group but also in the total black community.

The message to all those concerned with preventing alcohol abuse and alcoholism in the black community is that: (1) alcoholism can be deadly, and (2) alcoholism has costly psychological, emotional, economic, and health casualties in the black community that are too great to be borne. The crisis for the black community and black females especially is too great to await scientific answers. The condition is grave, and some answer must be forthcoming immediately. Certainly research needs in this area are tremendous, but some efforts must be employed now to try and turn this pattern around. The cost of error is not as great in the primary prevention stage as it would be in the secondary or tertiary stages. Human lives are at stake, we must act now.

REFERENCES

Bailey, M.P., Haberman, P.W., & Alksne, H. (1965). The epidemiology of alcoholism in an urban residential area. *Quarterly Journal of Studies on Alcohol, 26,* 19-40.

Bell, P., & Evans, J. (1983). Counseling the black alcoholic client. In T.D. Watts & R. Wright, Jr. (Eds.) *Black alcoholism: Toward a comprehensive understanding*. Springfield, Illinois: Charles C Thomas.

Bourne, P.G. (1973). Alcoholism in the urban negro population. In P.G. Bourne & F. Fox (Eds.) *Alcoholism: Progress in research and treatment*. New York: Academic Press.

Cahalan, D., & Cisin, I.H. (1968). American drinking practices: Summary of findings from a national probability sample. *Quarterly Journal of Studies on Alcohol, 29*, 130-151.

Cahalan, D., Cisin, I.H., & Crossley, H.M. (1969). *American drinking practices: A national study of drinking and attitudes*. New Brunswick, New Jersey: Rutgers Center of Alcohol Studies.

Clarke, J.I. (1978). *Self-esteem: A family affair*. Minneapolis, Minnesota: Winston Press.

Dawkins, M.P., Farrell, W.C., & Johnson, J.H. (1979). Spatial patterns of alcohol outlets in the Washington, D.C. black community. *Proceedings of the Pennsylvania Academy of Science*.

Gaines, J.J. (1976). Alcohol and the black woman. In F.D. Harper (Ed.) *Alcohol abuse and black America*. Alexandria, Virginia: Douglas Publishers.

Harper, F.D. (Ed.). (1976). *Alcohol abuse and black America*. Alexandria, Virginia: Douglas Publishers.

Harper, F.D. (1978). Alcohol use among North American blacks. In Y. Israel, F. Glaser, H. Kalant, R. Popham, W. Schmidt., & R. Smart (Eds.) *Research advances in alcohol and drug problems* (Vol. 4). New York: Plenum Publishers.

Haynes, M. (1975). The gap in health studies between black and white Americans. In R. Williams (Ed.) *Textbook of black related diseases*. New York: McGraw-Hill.

Keil, T.J. (1978). Sex role variations and women's drinking: Results from a household survey in Pennsylvania. *Journal of Studies in Alcohol, 39*(5), 859-868.

King, L.M. (1979). *Models of meaning and alcoholism in the black community*. Paper presented at Califorina Conference on Alcoholism. San Diego, California, 1-20.

Klatsky, A.L., Friedman, G.D., Seigelaut, A.B., & Gerard, M.J. (1977a). Alcohol consumption among white, black or oriental men and women: Kaiser Permanente Multiphasic Health examination data. *American Journal of Epidemiology, 105*(4), 311-323.

Knupfer, G. (1967). The epidemiology of problem drinking. *American Journal of Public Health, 57*, 973-986.

Kuller, L., Lilienfield, A., & Fisher, K. (1966). Sudden and unexpected deaths in young adults: An epidemiological study. *Journal of the American Medical Association, 198*, 248-252.

Leffall, L.D. (1975). Surgery and oncology. In R. Williams (Ed.) *Textbook of black related diseases*. New York: McGraw-Hill.

Locke, B.L., Kramer, M., & Pasamanick, B. (1960). Alcoholic psychoses among first admissions to public mental hospitals in Ohio. *Quarterly Journal of Studies in Alcohol, 21*, 457-474.

Lowenfish, S.K. (1977). Woman alcoholic: Her clinical and social emergence. *First International Action Conference on Substance Abuse*, Vol. I. Phoenix, Arizona, 68-84.

Miranda, V.L. (1983). Black alcohol prevention programming — past, present, future. In T. Watts & R. Wright (Eds.) *Black alcoholism: Toward a comprehensive understanding*. Springfield, Illinois: Charles C Thomas.

McAlpine, J. (1973). *Alcoholism and the black community*. Paper presented at the Workshop on Alcoholism Services to the Black community. Durham, North Caroline, November 11-14, 10.

McKirnan, D.J. (1978). Community perspectives on deviance: Some factors in the definition of alcohol abuse. *American Journal of Community Psychiatry, 6*, 219-238.

National Institute on Alcohol Abuse and Alcoholism. (1981). *First statistical compendium on alcohol and health*. Rockville, Maryland.

National Institute on Alcohol Abuse and Alcoholism: National Clearinghouse for Alcohol Information. (1979). *Blacks and alcohol: In brief*. Rockville, Maryland, The Institute.

Poussaint, A., & Atkinson, C. (1972). "Black youth and motivation." In R. L. Jones (Ed.) *Black psychology*. New York: Harper & Row Publishers.

Rimmer, J., Pitts, F., & Ninokur, G. (1971). Alcoholism, sex, socioeconomic status and race in two hospitalized samples. *Quarterly Journal of Studies on Alcohol, 32*, 942-952.

Robins, L.N., & Guze, S.B. (1971). Drinking practices and problems in the urban ghetto populations. In N.K. Mello & J.H. Mendelson (Eds.) *Recent advances in studies on alcoholism*. Washington, D.C.: U.S. Government Printing Office.

Rosenblatt, S.M., & Gross, M.M. (1971). Patients admitted for treatment of alcohol withdrawal syndromes: An epidemiological study. *Quarterly Journal of Studies on Alcohol, 32*, 104-115.

Sieber, M.H. (1979). Social background, attitudes and personality in a three year follow-up study on alcohol consumers. *Drug and Alcohol De-*

pendency, 4(5), 407-418.

Sterne, M.W., & Pittman, D. (1972). *Drinking patterns in the ghetto* (2 vols.) Mimeographed, 717 pages. St. Louis, Social Science Institute, Washington University.

Sterne, M.W. (1967). Drinking patterns and alcoholism among American negroes. In D. Pittman (Ed.) *Alcoholism.* New York: Harper & Row.

Strayer, R. (1962). A study of the negro alcoholic. *Quarterly Journal of Studies on Alcohol, 22,* 111-123.

United States Department of Health, Education and Welfare. (1978). In E.P. Noble (Ed.) *Third report to the United States Congress on Alcohol and Health,* DHEW Pub. No. (ADM) 79-832. Washington, D.C.: Supt. of Docs., U.S. Government Printing Office.

Viamontes, J.A., & Powell, B.J. (1974). Demographic characteristics of black and white male alcoholics. *International Journal of Addiction, 9,* 489-494.

Wall, J.H. (1937). "A Study of Alcoholism in Alcoholic Women," *Journal of Nervous and Mental Disorders,* Vol. 86, pp. 943-52.

Weschler, H., Dumone, H.W., & Gottlieb (1978). Drinking patterns of greater Boston adults: Subgroup differences on the QFU index. *Journal of Studies on Alcohol, 39*(7), 1158-1165.

Chapter 6

THE BLACK WOMAN,
ALCOHOL, AND PREVENTION:
AN EMPIRICAL EXPLORATION

BARBARA LYNN KAIL, D.S.W.

Problem and Background

A LCOHOLISM has been cited as one of the most serious, if not the most serious, problem facing the black community (Bourne & Light, 1979; Harper, 1976). Yet, little is known about drinking practices and attitudes toward alcohol within the black community. Even less is known about black women and alcohol. Our understanding of potential prevention strategies is woefully lacking. This study attempts to address the gap just described.

Qualitative studies suggest blacks may be a different subgroup with unique drinking patterns. Historically, patterns of alcohol use by blacks have differed from the white pattern emphasizing relatively heavy drinking during weekends, holidays, and festive occasions (Bourne & Light, 1979; Gaines, 1976; Watts & Wright, 1983). Lipscomb and Goddard (1984) describe drinking within the black community as generally occurring in a social setting with some ostentation. Individuals in this community may not readily recognize their own or other's problem drinking. They may also be less likely to recognize alcohol as a drug (Lipscomb & Goddard, 1984). Watts and Wright (1983) note that the unique ecological, environmental social and psychological experiences of blacks have resulted in culturally-patterned drinking behavior.

Quantitative studies of black drinking practices — particularly of black women — are almost nonexistent. Harper (1983) noted in 1977 that of 16,000 scientific articles published in the area of alcohol over a 30-year period, only 77 discussed alcohol and blacks. Only 11 of these 77 dealt primarily with a black population. None have focused primarily on black women (Harper, 1983).

The most widely cited finding on alcohol and the black woman suggests that black women may have particular difficulties with alcohol. Cahalan and Cisin (1968) reported that while black women were more likely to abstain from drinking, those who did drink, drank more heavily than their white counterparts. Recent research findings question this observation. Clark and Midanik (1982) report black women participating in their national survey are more likely to abstain than whites. However, among black women who drink, the percentage of heavy drinkers is comparable to that of other ethnic groups. Education, age, status as a female head of household and church attendance have also been related to drinking among black women (Cahalan & Cisin, 1968; Harper, 1983; King, 1985).

Prevention Models and the Black Woman

Even less is known about the prevention of alcohol problems and black women. However, four models of prevention have been proffered which might be applied to the problem at hand (Wilsnack, 1982).

- **Proscriptive**: This model views any alcohol use as problematic and proposes abstinence as the only viable prevention strategy.
- **Socialization**: Problematic alcohol use is perceived to be the result of inaccurate information and faulty attitudes regarding alcohol. Prevention efforts attempt to increase knowledge and change attitudes.
- **Control**: The availability and accessibility of alcohol is believed to predict problematic use of the substance. Advocates of this prevention model propose reducing per capita con-

sumption by restricting the availability of alcohol.

— **Public health**: This is a systems-oriented model which incorporates some features of the models described above (Catalano, 1979). The impact of three different systems on drinking behavior is evaluated. One system considered is the host, or the individual susceptible to drinking problems. Characteristics of these individuals and their relationships to drinking behavior are usually examined. A second system is that of the noxious agent, in this case alcohol. Patterns of availability, access and dissemination are considered. The third system is the enviornment. Here the focus is on the larger social norms, values, and settings which provide the context for drinking behavior.

Based on the public health model outlined above, this study proposes that black women may have some unique difficulties with alcohol and these difficulties may involve one or more of the following systems: host, access, and environmental context. Each of these systems and ensuing preventing strategies will be explored through a comparison of black and white women in the following areas:

1. How do black women differ from white women as hosts, in their access to alcohol, and the environmental context in which they drink? Each of the three systems described in the public health model will be considered in turn.

2. Only those who drink are "at risk" of developing problematic drinking practices. Given that a large percentage of the black female community may abstain, the identification of those most likely to use alcohol could be useful. Demographic predictors of alcohol use are therefore considered and compared to those of white women.

3. Finally, for those who may be "at risk" (black and white women who do not abstain) the relative salience of host characteristics, access and context are considered.

METHODOLOGY

This study is based upon a secondary analysis of data collected by L. Harris in January of 1974. A random multistage cluster sampling design was used to obtain a sample representative of the U.S. population eighteen years and older ($N = 1594$). The mere size of this sample makes it fertile ground for an analysis of subgroups such as black women. Both gender and age distributions of the sample as a whole are similar to census distributions (Martin, McDuffee & Presser, 1981). One potential sampling bias is the apparent underrepresentation of blacks in the sampling procedures employed (Martin, McDuffee & Pressor, 1981). Trained staff conducted face-to-face interviews with respondents in their homes. Although these data were collected over ten years ago, presenting some potential bias, this author is unaware of another more current and richer data set based on the sample of interest.

Available information included basic demographic information on: highest grade of school completed; age; household position and presence of children under eighteen. Respondents were also asked their religion and if they were an active member of their church or synagogue. A comparison of the 65 black female respondents and 652 white female respondents on these measures indicates these two samples differ in a few areas. Black respondents are less educated

TABLE 6-1
Demographic Comparison of Black and White Females

Demographics	White	Black	Significance Test
Percentage not graduated from high school	34.5	61.2	$\chi^2 = 19.95$**
Percentage under age 40	44.6	55.2	$\chi^2 = 2.81$
Percentage Protestant	64.2	92.5	$\chi^2 = 22.09$**
Percentage religiously active	50.1	53.0	$\chi^2 = .21$
Percentage female heads of households	27.2	32.8	$\chi^2 = .98$
Percentage no kids under 18	51.4	47.8	$\chi^2 = 2.09$

* p <.05
** p <.01

Measure	Description	Scoring
Host Drinking Practices	Those who indicated they drank were asked whether they engaged in the following behaviors frequently, sometimes, seldom or never: talking a lot about drinking; taking a drink at lunch time; taking more than 2 or 3 drinks at one sitting; taking a drink to feel better; going several days or weeks without drinking and then having several drinks at one time; getting sad when drinking; needing a drink to have fun; gulping drinks; showing the effects of liquor more quickly than most people; starting to drink without really thinking about it; slurring words or walking unsteadily after only a few drinks; drinking alone; getting belligerent after having a few drinks; taking a drink in the morning to relieve a hangover; forgetting what you did while drinking; keeping a bottle hidden for a quick pick-me-up. Responses to these questions were summed into a Likert scale.	Range = 0-47 (0 = abstainers); $\bar{x}$ = 11.48; Cronbach alpha = .83
Contact with other's drinking problems	Do you know anyone whose drinking interferes with the performance of his/her work?	1 = yes 2 = no
Knowledge of services	Do you know of any places in your community where people with a drinking problem can get help?	1 = yes 2 = no
Access Where drink	As far as your own drinking habits go, do you do most of your own drinking of alcoholic beverages at home, mostly at parties and other social functions, or do you drink mostly at taverns, bars or restaurants?	1 = don't drink; 2 = home; 3 = public places
Attendance at functions where alcohol is served	How often do you attend parties or other social occasions or business meetings where liquor is served?	4 = frequently; 3 = sometimes; 2 = seldom; 1 = never
Environmental context Perception of alcohol as a drug	Responses to the following items were summed into a Likert scale: Alcohol is a drug; drunkenness is like an overdose of drugs; the host who encourages heavy drinking can be described as a drug pusher.	Range = 3.7; $\bar{x}$ = 4.803; Cronbach alpha = .49
Perception of alcohol as a problematic substance	Respondents were asked if heavy drinking of alcoholic beverages and drunken driving were problems. Responses were summed into a Likert scale.	Range = 2-7; $\bar{x}$ = 6.35; Cronbach alpha = .57

Figure 6-1. Measures of Host Characteristics, Access and Environmental Context

Figure 6-1 *(continued)*

| Perception of the alcoholic as different | Respondents were asked the extent to which the following statements were basically true, partially true, or mostly false: No one turns into an alcoholic unless he is unhappy to begin with; it takes years of heavy drinking before becoming an alcoholic; no one with a good moral or religious background becomes an alcoholic; if a person drinks too much, it's because they are under pressure; a person is an alcoholic only if he gives up eating regularly and taking care of his health. | Range = 5–15; x̄ = 7.65; Cronbach alpha = .67 |

than their white counterparts (see Table 6-1). All but one of these black women are Protestant, a higher percentage than their white counterparts. Black respondents did not differ from their white counterparts in household composition. About half of each group have children under eighteen. About one third of each group are female heads of household. This last finding does not appear to be in line with current census data which indicate black women are more likely to head a household than are white women (Levitan & Belous, 1981).

Measures for each of the posited systems within the public health prevention framework (host, access and environmental context) were developed from the available information. Figure 6-1 describes these measures.

Some of these concepts have been more successfully measured than others. A clearer measure of actual alcohol consumption in terms of frequency, quantity, and type would have been most desirable. Several characteristics of the host are lacking in these data, including better measures of contact with problematic drinkers and parental drinking practices. The measurement of access to alcohol is relatively weak. The items used in the analysis below are only poor proxies for the concept of interest. Items measuring the distribution of retail outlets for alcohol in the respondent's neighborhood would have been preferable. An item measuring whether alcohol is kept in the home would also have been useful.

However, even given the sampling and measurement limitations described above, the data base still provides an opportunity to explore an area that is virtually uncharted.

TABLE 6-2
Comparison of Black and White Female on Public Health Systems

Public Health System	White	Black	Significance Test
Host			
Percentage know person whose drinking interferes with work	32.2	31.8	$\chi^2 = .00$
Percentage know where to go in community for alcohol problems	45.0	25.8	$\chi^2 = 9.14**$
Percentage abstaining	49.0	62.1	$\chi^2 = 4.16*$
Access			
Percentage drink public places	35.8	18.2	$\chi^2 = 8.28**$
Percentage never attend social events where liquor served	28.3	40.3	$\chi^2 = 10.97**$
Environmental Context			
Mean score perception of alcohol as problem	6.44	6.54	$t = -.82$
Mean score perception of alcohol as drug	4.79	5.11	$t = -3.28**$
Mean score perception of alcoholics as different	7.66	8.03	$t = -1.30$

*$p < .05$
**$p < .01$

FINDINGS

A Comparison of Black and White Women

A first question is: What are the unique aspects of the black woman's encounter with alcohol? How do black respondents differ from white respondents as hosts, in their access to alcohol, and the environmental context they drink in?

Black respondents do differ from white respondents as hosts. Black women in this sample are significantly more likely to abstain completely from alcohol. In fact, almost two-thirds state they do not drink. Black women are also less likely to know where to go in the community should help with drinking problems be needed (see Table 6-2).

Black women in this sample have significantly less access to alcohol compared to their white counterparts. White respondents are more likely to attend social events where liquor is served and are more likely to drink in public (see Table 6-2).

There are also ethnic differences in the norms surrounding alcohol use. Black respondents are more likely to perceive alcohol as a drug compared to white respondents. There are no differences in perception of alcoholics or perception of alcohol use as a national problem.

Predictors of Drinking

Given the high proportion of abstainers in both the black (62.1%) and white (49.0%) samples, a next logical question is: What will predict those who drink? This is the audience at which prevention efforts need to be aimed.

A multiple regression analysis of various demographic characteristics on the drinking measure indicates education and religious activities may be important predictors (see Table 6-3). The relatively uneducated and religiously active black women in this sample are most likely to abstain. White women in this sample most likely to abstain are also relatively less educated and more religiously active; they are also relatively older.

Predictors of Problematic Drinking

Of those who drink, black respondents do not report more problematic drinking practices compared to their white counterparts (t = -.83 ns).

For these respondents who drink — who may be at risk of developing problematic drinking practices — a closer examination of the three systems in the public health model may be useful. Which system(s) is most predictive of problematic drinking? Are these systems

Prevention of Black Alcoholism

TABLE 6-3
Demographic Predictors of Drinking

Predictor	Blacks N = 65 R^2=.18*	Whites N = 652 R^2=.12**
	Standardized Beta Weight	Standardized Beta Weight
Age	.00	-.16**
Education	.33**	.20**
Religiously active	-.26*	-.16**
Number of children	-.02	.04
Female heads of household	.03	-.02

+ p< .10
* p< .05
** p< .01

differentially salient for the two ethnic groups? Table 6-4 presents measures of the three systems regressed on the drinking measure, for those who drink.

The variables included in this analysis are only minimally predictive of problematic drinking practices for black respondents (R^2 = .51 p< .07). Drinking in public is predictive as is the perception of alcoholics as different from oneself (see Table 6-4).

For white respondents, the prediction appears to be stronger (R^2 = .06 p< .05). Those who frequently attend social events where liquor is served are more likely to report problematic drinking practices. Minimizing the problem alcohol may hold for this country is also predictive of problematic drinking practices. Findings concerning the perception of alcoholics are interesting. While black respondents who perceive alcoholics as different are more likely to report problems, the findings for white women are just the opposite. Those who see alcoholics as similar to other individuals are more likely to report problems (see Table 6-4).

TABLE 6-4
Public Health Predictors of Problematic Drinking Behavior

	Blacks N = 24 $R^2=.51$	Whites N = 310 $R^2=.06*$
	Standardized Beta Weight	Standardized Beta Weight
Know person whose drinking interferes with work	-.36	-.10
Know where to go in community for problem with alcohol	.33	-.04
Drink in public places	-.46*	.01
Attend social events where liquor is served	.17	.13*
Perception of alcohol as problem	-.01	-.12*
Perception of alcohol as drug	-.23	.01
Perception of alcoholics as different	.52**	-.11*

p<.10
*p<.05
**p<.001

DISCUSSION

To return to the first question posed in this study, the data suggest there may be some differences between black and white women as hosts, in their access to.alcohol, and the environmental context in which alcohol is used. Black women in this sample are more likely to abstain and are less likely to be aware of community resources for alcohol treatment. Black respondents also seem to have less access to alcohol — they are less likely to go to social functions where alcohol is served and less likely to drink in public. Finally, black women in this sample are more likely to see alcohol as a drug. None of these findings is particularly surprising, given the little that is known in this area. Compared to white respondents, black respondents then appear to be less at risk of developing problematic drinking practices, given their limited drinking, restricted access and awareness of alcohol. However, when they do encounter alcohol-related difficulties, they are less likely to know of sources of help.

Those women most likely to abstain appear to be similar in both the black and white communities; they are relatively less educated and participate more actively in religious institutions. These findings are in line with those cited by King (1985). The findings also support Clark and Midanik (1982). Black respondents who did drink did not have higher scores on the problematic drinking scale compared to their white counterparts.

These data do appear to support the assertion that there may be some salient differences between black and white women in the predictors of problematic drinking. Prediction for the black respondents is minimal, perhaps because of the very small sample size. It appears that those who have greater access to alcohol and those who see alcoholics as intrinsically different from themselves are more likely to encounter difficulties. Prediction for white respondents is stronger. Again, availability affects the likelihood of problematic drinking. The environmental context poses a most interesting picture. For white respondents those who see alcoholics as similar to themselves are most likely to encounter problems — just the opposite of the black respondents.

Implications for Prevention

The findings described above appear to have some implications for the public health model of prevention developed above. If black women are less aware of community resources, agencies in the black community may need to make special outreach efforts. Those women who do drink in public may be especially at risk, and they might be the target of some special efforts.

Ethnic differences in the perception of the alcoholic, suggested by the findings reported above, raise some very interesting issues in

prevention. Black women who engage in problematic drinking practices are more likely to perceive alcoholics to be different from themselves. This could be an indicator of possibly two processes. The first
is one of denial in the face of great stigma — especially given the relatively large proportion of their sisters who are teetotalers. A second
variation on this theme is proposed by some authors who suggest the
black community may be more tolerant of problematic drinking
(e.g. Lipscomb & Goddard, 1984). The perception of alcoholics as
different may indicate an unwillingness or reluctance to "label" such
individuals; the line at which heavy drinking becomes deviant is
further away.

In either case, the black woman who drinks problematically may
encounter more difficulties than her white counterpart. If she is
denying her problem, she will be less likely to seek treatment. Once
enrolled in largely male-oriented programs she may experience even
greater stigma, although overall blacks tend to do better in treatment than whites (Bentley, 1978). If the findings indicate a greater
tolerance of drinking, the black woman who drinks is exposed to yet
another set of difficulties. Given the reluctance to define someone as
having a drinking problem, once an individual is so designated she
may encounter greater stigma. She may find herself distanced even
further than her white counterpart from crucial networks in church,
family, and community.

It appears that the prevention tactic of choice within the black
community has been proscription. Black churches have traditionally
followed fundamentalist beliefs condemning all drinking (Bourne &
Light 1979). The high proportion of black women who abstain and
their greater church attendance bear witness to the observation
made above. This emphasis on the substance alcohol is useful and
may have an impact on the perception of alcohol as a drug and
awareness of the difficulties problematic drinking practices pose for
the community. However, such tactics concentrate only on one system, neglecting the host and the environmental context. The findings described above suggest that several systems have an impact on
drinking practices. Churches might be advised to consider a more
holistic view of the problem, addressing the community's lack of
knowledge and attitudes concerning those who do drink. Indeed,
several authors have suggested recruiting churches specifically to assist in prevention tactics (e.g. Miranda, 1983).

Future Research

Research into the difficulties alcohol poses for the black community and in particular the black woman is urgently needed. A first step would be to develop data based on larger more representative samples of blacks. Measures need to be refined. In particular, measures of drinking practices should at a minimum include frequency of drinking, amount drunk at each sitting, and type of beverage. Finally, this study only begins to touch on the issue of the problematic female drinker. Typically, these women, and in particular these black women, have been treated as one monolithic group. Yet, one questions whether this is the case, or whether there are distinguishable subgroups of black women who drink problematically. These issues remain largely unexplored.

REFERENCES

Bentley, J.T. (1978). The relationship of psychiatric and demographic variables to the success of alcoholics in treatment. *Dissertation Abstracts International*, 39 (4), 2059a.

Bourne, P.G. & Light, E. (1979). Alcohol problems in Blacks and women. In J.H. Mendelson & N.K. Mello (Eds.), *The diagnosis and treatment of alcoholism* (pp. 83-123) New York: McGraw Hill, 1979.

Cahalan, D. & Cisin, I.H. (1968). American drinking practices: summary of findings from a national probability sample. *Quarterly Journal of Studies on Alcohol*, 29, 130-151.

Catalano, R. (1979). *Health behavior and the community*. New York: Pergamon Press.

Clark, W. B. & Midanik, L. (1982). Alcohol use and alcohol problems among U.S. adults. In *Alcohol consumption and related problems* (Alcohol and Health Monograph #1). Rockville, Md.: National Institute on Alcohol Abuse and Alcoholism.

Gaines, J.J. (1976). Alcohol and the Black woman. In F.D. Harper (Ed.), *Alcohol abuse and Black America* (pp. 153-162). Alexandria, Va.: Douglas Publishers.

Harper, F.D. (1976). Overview: alcohol and Blacks. In F.D. Harper (Ed.), *Alcohol abuse and Black America* (pp. 1-12) Alexandria, Va.: Douglas Publishers.

Harper, F.D. (1983). Alcohol use and alcoholism among Black Americans. In T.D. Watts & R. Wright (Eds.), *Black alcoholism* (pp. 19-36). Springfield, Ill.: Charles C Thomas.

King, L.M. (1983). Alcoholism: studies regarding Black Americans. In T.D. Watts & R. Wright (Eds.), *Black alcoholism* (pp. 37-63). Springfield, Ill.: Charles C Thomas.

King, S. (1985). Black females and alcoholism prevention strategies. In R. Wright & T.D. Watts (1983). *Black alcoholism*. Springfield, Ill.: Charles C Thomas.

Levitan, S.A. & Belous, R.S. (1981). *What's happening to the American family*. Baltimore: Johns Hopkins.

Lipscomb, W.R. & Goddard, L.L. (1984). Black family features and drinking behavior. *Journal of Drug Issues, 2*, 337-347.

Martin, E., McDuffee, D. & Presser, S (1981). *Sourcebook of Harris National Surveys: Repeated Questions 1963-1976*. University of North Carolina at Chapel Hill: Institute for Research in Social Sciences.

Miranda, V.L. (1983). Black alcohol prevention programming — past, present and future. In T.D. Watts & R. Wright (Eds.), *Black alcoholism* (pp. 162-173). Springfield, Ill.: Charles C Thomas.

Watts, T.D. & Wright, R. (1983). Discussion. In T.D. Watts & R. Wright (Eds.), *Black alcoholism* (pp. 5-18). Springfield, Ill.: Charles C Thomas.

Wilsnack, S.C. (1982). Prevention of alcohol problems in women. In *Alcohol and Health: special population issues* (Alcohol and Health Monograph #4). Rockville, Md.: National Institute on Alcohol Abuse and Alcoholism.

Chapter 7

DRINKING PATTERNS AMONG BLACK
AND NONBLACK ADOLESCENTS:
RESULTS OF A NATIONAL SURVEY

Thomas C. Harford, Ph.D.

ALCOHOL ABUSE is regarded as one of the greater health problems of the black community in the United States (Bourne & Light, 1979; Harper, 1976). Cirrhosis mortality rates are disproportionately high among black Americans. Rates among black men and women, aged 25 to 34, are several times higher than for white men and women of the same age. For all age groups up to 65 years of age, the cirrhosis mortality rate for black Americans is nearly twice that for white Americans. When examining racial differences in cirrhosis mortality rates, it is important to acknowledge the potential contributions made by such factors as nutritional differences, genetic differences, bias in recording information on death certificates and psychosocial differences. While alcohol is not the exclusive cause of cirrhosis of the liver, prolonged heavy drinking is recognized as a major contributor.

High cirrhosis rates in the black population are a historically new phenomenon. They did not begin to exceed rates in the general population until the late 1950s. Herd (1983) has shown that the abrupt rise in cirrhosis mortality among blacks in the late 1950s and 1960s was in part a reflection of a transformation in black drinking patterns initiated at the turn of the century and the massive population shifts which began at that time. The increase in cirrhosis mortality among black cohorts born in the early decades of this century are strongest in the high urban areas which were the major centers of black migration over the past century.

Although cirrhosis mortality rates are disproportionately high among black Americans, yet, in one important segment of the black population, high school students, alcohol abuse and even use are at relatively low levels.

In a review of the 1960-75 literature, Blane and Hewitt (1977) noted that the majority of studies of alcohol use among black adolescents were derived from surveys of high school students. These surveys indicated lower rates of lifetime as well as current alcohol use among black high school students compared to nonblack students. While many of these surveys are limited by small subgroup sizes and nonrandom samples of students, several national surveys support these findings. The 1974 national survey of junior and senior high school students (Rachel et al., 1975) indicated that black students had the smallest proportion of current drinkers when compared to white and other ethnic/racial groups of students. Blacks also had the lowest proportions of moderate and heavy drinkers. These findings were also replicated in the 1978 national survey of senior high school students (Rachal et al., 1980). In a national household survey on drug abuse, Fishburne, Abelson, and Cisin (1979) reported that approximately 38 percent of white respondents, age 12-17 years, were current drinkers compared to 20 percent among black and other races. Similar findings were reported for the years 1972, 1974, 1976, and 1977.

Several explanations may be offered to account for the lower prevalence of alcohol use among black high school students. Surveys of adolescent alcohol use, while indicating that older students drink more than younger students and that boys drink more than girls, also have shown that other demograhic variables relate to alcohol use in this population (Rachal et al., 1975). Lower levels of alcohol consumption have been reported for teenagers living in southern geographic regions, those affiliated with Protestant religious denominations, and those that attain higher academic status in school work (Rachal et al., 1975; Blane & Hewitt, 1977). The conservative or fundamentalist Protestant upbringing of many blacks, for example, may be an important factor in accounting for the differences in drinking levels among black and nonblack youth. These and other demographic variations in the samples of black and nonblack students may account for the differences in alcohol use reported by these students in surveys. A few studies, however, indicate that differences between black and nonblack youth in drinking prevalence persist when demographic factors are controlled (Backman et al., 1981; Harford et al., 1982).

A second explanation for differences in drinking prevalence between these two groups of students relates to differences in underreporting of alcohol consumption. Blacks, as members of a minority group, may withhold or underreport their use of alcohol in national surveys. This is a reasonable point, especially for black students in predominately white schools or white neighborhoods. The national surveys on drug abuse, however, revealed little variation in the use of the illicit drugs among white and black respondents aged 12 to 17 years. It seems unlikely that blacks would conceal the use of alcohol but not other illicit drugs. Moreover, Harford, Lowman, and Kaelber (1982) examined the drinking patterns of black students in predominantly white schools and black students in predominantly black schools. It was hypothesized that black students in predominantly black schools would be less likely to withhold information on drinking practices than would black students in predominantly white schools. Statistical analyses of beverage specific consumption were not significant. There was no evidence of selective underreporting of alcohol consumption. Nor was there evidence of variations in the self-reports of the frequency of the use of marijuana between black and white students.

A third explanation relates to the fact that surveys of school populations exclude the school dropouts, and these dropouts have been shown to have higher levels of problems associated with alcohol (Cockerham, 1975; MacKay, Phillips & Bryce, 1967). Studies of institutionalized, delinquent, and school dropout populations, however, are inconsistent with respect to patterns of alcohol use among white and black teenagers — some reported lower rates of problem drinking among blacks, others reported higher rates, and others reported no differences (Blane & Hewitt, 1977). In addition, the U.S. Bureau of the Census (1981) figures indicate that white dropout rates are similar to or slightly higher than black rates up to 18 years of age. At 18, school dropout rates for black males and females begin to increase steeply and to exceed rates for white students.

A fourth explanation may be found in variables which differentiate exposure to and involvement with alcohol among black and nonblack students. Harford, Lowman, and Kaelber (1982) noted that the onset of drinking was grade-related among black students but was characterized by a later onset relative to nonblack students. A delay in the exposure to alcohol may underlie the reported differences in drinking prevalence. Other studies, however, suggest a commonality of drinking correlates among both black and nonblack students. Jessor and his colleagues have developed a comprehensive network of variables encompassing personality, the percieved environment, and behavior patterns that account for over 50 percent of the variance in adolescent involvement in problem drinking and marijuana use (Donovan & Jessor, 1978; Jessor & Jessor, 1977; Jessor, Chase, & Donovan, 1980). Their system of variables has been shown to constitute psychosocial risk for problem behavior in subsamples of adolescents differing in gender and ethnic background. Despite the fact that similar predictors of drinking may apply to both racial/ethnic groups, little is known about the processes underlying the differences in drinking prevalence for these two groups.

The overall objective of this study was to identify factors which relate to the use of alcohol within each of these racial/ethnic student groups. The 1978 national survey (Rachal et al., 1980) was limited to senior high school students and the overall sample of black students was 496. The present study draws upon the earlier 1974 national survey (Rachal et al., 1975) which encompassed a wider age spectrum and a larger sample of black students.

MATERIALS AND METHODS

Data for the present study were obtained from a 1974 cross-sectional survey of a nationwide probability sample of all junior and junior high school students in grades 7-12 in the contiguous 48 States and in the District of Columbia (Rachal et al., 1975). A stratified two-stage sample was used. The primary sampling frame was stratified by census regions, by community size, and by ethnic characteristics. A sample of 50 primary sampling units (PSU's) consisting of counties or groups of counties was chosen within each selected PSU, the number of homerooms and the number of students enrolled were determined for each of the six grades, either for all schools (rural areas) or for a sample of schools (metropolitan area). The homerooms were stratified into three grade strata: grade 7-8, 9-10, 11-12. A sample of approximately five homerooms per grade stratum was selected within each of the 50 PSU's. A self-administered, 35-page questionnaire was completed by students in the cooperating classes in the sample during the regular school hours at the school facilities. Useable questionnaires were completed by 13,122 students from 643 classrooms. Of the original 717 classes in the sample, 223 (31.1%) were lost because cooperation could not be obtained from State or local school officials. The overall response rate was 72.7 percent including replacement classrooms.

The present analysis compared students who indicated in the questionnaire that they were "Black," not of Hispanic origin ($N = 930$) and all other nonblack students ($N = 12,192$).

Measures of alcohol consumption were obtained from beverage specific estimates of the typical frequency of alcohol use (every day, 3-4 days a week, 1-2 days a week, 3-4 days a month, once a month, less than once a month but at least once a year, less than once a year, never) and from beverage specific estimates of the number of drinks consumed per typical occasion (12 or more, about 9, 6, 5, 4, 3, 2, 1, less than 1, do not drink).

The beverage specific quantity-frequency information was used to estimate overall frequency (most frequently used beverage) and overall quantity (highest beverage amount).

In addition to alcohol information, the questionnaire contained several items of relevance to alcohol use. The items are organized into the following sets of variables: demography, drinking models, attitudes, and behaviors. Item descriptions and mean scores for the samples of nonblack and black students are presented in Table 1.

Demographic factors included gender, grade in school, an index of socioeconomic status using a combination of parents' occupation and education, geographic region, religious affiliation, family intactness (both parents in household), number of older siblings, number of younger siblings, size of peer network ("How many kids do you hang around with?"), and number of older peers.

TABLE 7-1

Variable Description and Mean Scores for Samples of
Black and Non-Black Students

Demographic	Item Description	Non-Blacks (N = 12,192)	Blacks (N = 930)	t-test
Gender	boys = 1; girls = 2	1.52 (0)†	1.52 (0)	0.49
Grade in school	7th through 12th	9.35 (0)	9.28 (0)	0.95
Socioeconomic index	low = 0; high = 9	6.23 (0)	5.44 (0)	10.40**
Region	non-South = 1; South = 2	1.27 (0)	1.35 (0)	5.48**
Religious affiliation	Baptist/Methodist = 1; other = 2	1.74 (916)	1.33 (123)	25.56**
Family intactness	both parents = 1; other = 2	1.21 (312)	1.41 (65)	14.26**
Number of older siblings	none = 2; twelve = 14	3.97 (1150)	4.89 (99)	12.04**
Number of younger siblings	none = 2; twelve = 14	3.66 (1755)	4.34 (153)	10.18**
Number of peers	none = 1; nine or more = 10	5.99 (98)	5.95 (5)	0.50
Number of older peers	none = 1; older = 2	1.14 (197)	1.19 (22)	4.05**
Drinking Models				
Parental drinking	both = 1; one = 2; none = 3	1.83 (416)	1.95 (79)	5.07**
School peers drinking	none = 1; all = 5	3.24 (268)	2.77 (76)	12.71**
Friends drinking	none = 1; all = 5	3.05 (263)	2.54 (77)	10.57**
Attitudes				
Social effects	not important = 1; important = 4	2.71 (449)	2.37 (96)	9.54**
Status reasons	not important = 1; important = 4	1.87 (494)	1.96 (108)	2.84*
Personal effects	not important = 1; important = 4	1.88 (501)	1.99 (107)	3.86**
Conforming reasons	not important = 1; important = 4	1.94 (559)	1.85 (113)	2.51*
Behaviors				
Academic grades	A's = 1; D's and F's = 7	3.32 (0)	3.79 (0)	9.45**
Religiosity	low = 5; high = 20	13.54 (670)	14.70 (182)	8.00**
Access to alcohol	no = 1; always = 4	2.34 (1242)	1.77 (151)	14.14**
Amount of spending money	none = 1; more than $11 = 5	2.99 (85)	3.09 (4)	2.28*
Extent of deviant behavior	low = 12; high = 48	17.61 (705)	16.80 (139)	3.94**
Marijuana frequency	none = 1; eleven or more = 12	2.97 (718)	2.82 (116)	1.13

† Figures within parentheses indicate number of missing cases.
* p < .01
** p < .001

The influence of drinking models was assessed by three items which included parental drinking (1 = one or both drink regularly, 2 = none or both drink sometimes, 3 = parents do not drink), number of kids in school who drink (1 = none to 5 = all of them), and number of kids you hang around with drinking (1 = none to 5 = all of them).

Attitudes related to drinking assessed the overall importance of drinking in each of the following areas: (1) social effects ("to have a good time"; "it's a good way to celebrate"); (2) status functions ("people think you've been around if you drink"; "it's part of becoming an adult"); (3) personal effects ("when there are too many pressures on me"; "makes things like doing well in school seem less important"; "keeps my mind off problems") (4) conforming functions ("not to be different from the rest of the kids"; "to be a part of the group").

Behavioral factors include academic grades, religiosity (a five-item scale of the importance placed upon religious teachings, practice, and counsel for the direction of daily life developed by Rohrbaugh & Jessor, 1975), ease of access to alcohol, amount of spending money, extent of deviant behavior (based on a twelve-item scale developed by Jessor & Jessor, 1977, assessing involvement in stealing, fighting, property destruction, truancy and other transgressions), and number of times the student reported using marijuana in the past 6 months.

RESULTS

Among the sample of black students, 33.3 percent of the boys and 43.2 percent of the girls reported that they either abstained from the use of alcohol or drank less than once a year. Abstinence and infrequent drinking were lower for nonblack students. About 23 percent of the boys and 30.8 percent of the girls abstained or drank less than once a year. Overall, 38 percent of black students and 27 percent of nonblack students abstained or drank less than once a year.

While the proportion of abstainers is high among black students, Harford et al. (1982) have indicated that alcohol use is grade-related among both black and nonblack students. Figure 7-1 presents the proportions of students in the 1974 survey who reported drinking once a month or more by grade and ethnic/racial group. The figure indicates that the onset of drinking among black students is grade related, as it is among nonblack students, but that the onset of drinking is delayed among blacks in grades seven through nine. It is important, then, to examine the nature of the differences both within and between each of the two ethnic/racial groups.

Statistical analyses of the variables under study in Table 7-1 indicated that the sample of black students differed significantly from the nonblack sample on most of the variables.

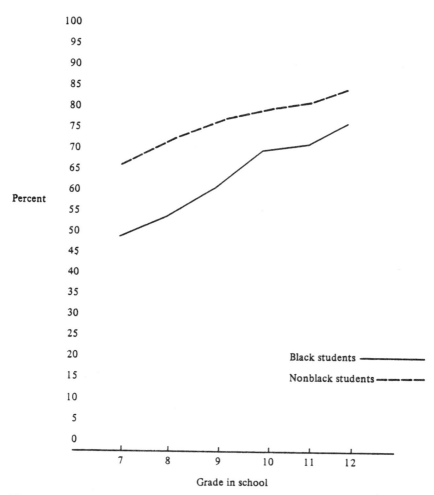

Figure 7-1. Proportion of students who report drinking alcohol once a month or more by grade and ethnic/racial group

Comparisons between the two groups revealed that blacks did not differ from nonblacks with regard to gender or grade in school. Blacks were of lower socioeconomic status, of Baptist/Methodist affiliations, from less intact families, from families with greater numbers of both older and younger siblings (larger families), and older peer networks.

In addition to differences in demographic characteristics associated with socioeconomic status, there were significant differences with respect to the alcohol-related variables. Blacks, when compared to nonblacks, reported less parental drinking and less drinking among both school peers and friends.

With regard to the importance of attitudes related to drinking, blacks rated social and conforming factors as less important reasons for drinking and status and personal effects as slightly more important than did nonblacks.

Blacks did less well academically and were higher on religiosity scores. They had less access to alcohol, slightly more spending money, and less deviant behavior patterns. The overall direction of these differences are such as to expect a lower drinking prevalence among black students. Blacks, for example, reported fewer drinking models, placed less importance on reasons for drinking, and had less access to alcohol than did nonblacks. Black students, while indicating poorer academic performance than nonblack students, had higher religiosity scores and less involvement in deviant behavior patterns. Consistent with other studies, however, black students did not differ from nonblack students with regard to the use of marijuana.

Table 7-2 presents the mean scores by drinker status (abstainer versus drinker) within each of the two samples for each of the variables under investigation. One-way analyses of variance for the four groups (drinker status by racial/ethnic group) were significant (p .01) on every variable. Table 7-2 also indicates significant differences associated with planned comparisons within the four groups. Of initial concern are the differences within each of the two ethnic/racial groups.

Among the nonblack sample, the majority of variables were significantly related to drinker status. Drinkers, compared to abstainers, were more likely to be boys, older, of higher socioeconomic

TABLE 7-2

Mean Scores on Demographic and Alcohol-related Variables for
Samples of Black and Non-Black Students

| Demographic | Non-Black Students | | Black Students | | Comparisons | | |
	Abstainers (1)	Drinkers (2)	Abstainers (3)	Drinkers (4)	(1) (2)	(3) (4)	(1) (3)	(2) (4)
Gender	1.59	1.49**	1.59	1.48	**	**	NS	NS
Grade in school	8.81	9.55**	8.88	9.55	**	**	NS	NS
Socioeconomic index	5.94	6.34**	5.31	5.51	**	NS	**	**
Region	1.35	1.24**	1.38	1.34	**	NS	NS	**
Religious affiliation	1.64	1.78**	1.31	1.35	**	NS	**	**
Family intactness	1.19	1.21*	1.39	1.42	*	NS	**	**
Number of older siblings	4.02	3.95	5.18	4.71	NS	*	**	**
Number of younger siblings	3.75	3.62**	4.49	4.24	**	NS	**	**
Number of peers	5.53	6.17**	5.84	6.03	**	NS	NS	NS
Number of older peers	1.09	1.16**	1.16	1.22	**	*	**	**
Drinking Models								
Parental drinking	2.17	1.70**	2.13	1.84	**	**	NS	**
School peers drinking	2.69	3.44**	2.36	3.04	**	**	**	**
Friends drinking	1.96	3.46**	1.88	2.96	**	**	NS	**
Attitudes								
Social effects	2.09	2.93**	2.01	2.59	**	**	NS	**
Status reasons	1.85	1.88	1.91	2.00	NS	NS	NS	*
Personal effects	1.85	1.89*	2.01	1/98	NS	NS	*	NS
Conforming reasons	1,83	1.98**	1.83	1.86	**	NS	NS	NS
Behaviors								
Academic grades	3.11	3.40**	3.63	3.89	**	*	**	**
Religiosity	15.21	12.93**	15.47	14.20	**	**	NS	**
Access to alcohol	1.53	2.66**	1.47	2.19	**	**	NS	**
Amount of spending money	2.61	3.14**	2.85	3.24	**	**	**	NS
Extent of deviant behavior	14.50	18.70**	14.90	18.09	**	**	NS	*
Marijuana frequency	1.20	3.60**	1.32	3.79	**	**	NS	NS

* $p < .001$
** $p < .01$

status, from nonsouthern regions and of nonBaptist/nonMethodist religious affiliation. Drinkers tended to be from less intact families (one or more parents absent), had fewer younger siblings, a greater number of peer networks, and more older peers.

Drinkers, compared to abstainers, reported greater models for drinking, placed greater importance on social and conforming reasons for drinking, greater access to alcohol, greater involvement in general deviant behavior and marijuana use, and less involvement in general deviant behavior and marijuana use, and less involvement in religion and school performance. These findings are consistent with the results obtained by Jessor and his colleagues in studies of adolescent problem drinking.

Within the sample of black students, black drinkers tended to be boys and older in age. Unlike nonblack drinkers, however, there were few other demographic differences between black abstainers and drinkers. There was a tendency for black drinkers to have fewer older siblings and to have a greater number of older companions in their peer group.

A pattern similar to that of nonblacks emerged with respect to drinking models, attitudes, and behaviors. Black drinkers, compared to black abstainers, reported greater models for drinking, placed more importance on the social effects of drinking, greater access to alcohol, greater involvement in general deviant behavior and marijuana use, and less involvement in religion and school performance.

These results indicates a similar pattern of the correlates of drinker status among both black and nonblack students with respect to the alcohol-related variables.

In order to assess the relative contributions of these variables with respect to drinker status, particularly those associated with demographic factors related to socioeconomic class, a discriminant function analysis was conducted separately for each student group. Because of the larger number of missing cases associated with some of the variables, their inclusion would drastically reduce the sample size for multivariate analysis. This is especially critical in view of the number of black students in the sample. For this reason, several of the variables were omitted from the analysis. The majority of these variables related to demographic factors, factors shown to be non-

TABLE 7-3

Standardized Discriminant Function Coefficients Among
Samples of Black and Non-Black Students

Demographic	Non-Black Students (N = 9,268)	Black Students (N = 530)
Gender	–06	–10
Grade in school	NS	.20
Socioeconomic index	.03	NS
Region	-12	NS
Religious affiliation		
Family intactness		
Number of older siblings		
Number of younger siblings		
Number of peers	04	NS
Number of older peers	NS	.13
Drinking Models		
Parental drinking	–29	–28
Friends drinking	41	41
Attitudes		
Social effects	32	42
Status reasons	NS	NS
Personal effects	–09	NS
Conforming reasons	–05	–27
Behaviors		
Academic grades	02	NS
Religiosity	–09	–13
Access to alcohol	32	.09
Amount of spending money	07	25
Extent of deviant behavior	20	26
Marijuana frequency	–07	NS

significant in the univariate tests with black students. The one exception to the demographic factors was access to alcohol. Because of its theoretical content, the discriminant analyses were conducted with this variable included. Its inclusion reduced the sample size of black students available for analysis from 594 to 530. Comparable results were obtained with the "access to alcohol" variable. The standardized discriminant function coefficients for black and non-black students are presented in Table 7-3. These coefficients reflect the relative contributions of each variable controlling for the effects of all other variables. The canonical correlations in both analyses were highly significant (p .001) both for blacks (.569) and nonblacks (.540). The results from the two analyses yield very similar findings. Among both black and nonblack samples, the major variables distinguishing abstainers and drinkers were parents' drinking, friends' drinking, importance of social effects of drinking, extent of deviant behavior, and amount of spending money. Grade in school, conforming reasons for drinking, and amount of spending money made relatively high contributions in the black student sample. Access to alcohol made a substantial contribution in the nonblack sample.

In order to assess the relative contributions of these factors with regard to the frequency of drinking and the number of drinks per typical occasion, the same set of variables used in the discriminant analysis was used in multiple regression.

Measures of the typical frequency of alcohol use and of the number of drinks consumed per typical occasion were regressed in a stepwise fashion on the set of predictor variables. The regressions were done separately for nonblack and black students, and the standardized regression coefficients (Beta) are presented in Table 7-4.

Each coefficient reflects the effects of a particular variable after the effects of the others are controlled. Among black students, the following variables were related to the frequency of drinking: gender, friends' drinking, social effects, access to alcohol, amount of spending money, extent of deviant behavior, and marijuana frequency. More frequent drinking occurred among boys and among students with drinking friends, access to alcohol, greater involvement in deviant behavior and use of marijuana, more spending money, and attitudes viewing the social effects of alcohol as important. These same variables were significant among nonblack students. In addition, the following variables were also significant for nonblack students: grade in school, number of peers, parental drinking, conforming reasons for drinking, academic grades, and religiosity.

Among both samples of nonblack and black students, the following variables were significantly related to the amount of consumption: gender, grade in school, friends' drinking, social effects, access to alcohol, extent of deviant behavior, and marijuana frequency. Heavier consumption occurred among boys and older students and students with drinking friends, attitudes viewing social effects of alcohol as important, access to alcohol, greater involvement in deviant behavior and more frequent use of marijuana. In addition, the fol-

TABLE 7-4
Standardized Regression Coefficients (Beta) Predicting
Drinking Frequency and Drinking Quantity Among
Non-Black and Black Students

Demographic	Frequency		Quantity	
	Non-Black	Black	Non-Black	Black
Gender	−.07*	.08*	.12*	.06*
Grade in school	.04*	.00	−04*	−10*
Socioeconomic	.00	.04	05*	.02
Region	.00	.04	01*	.03
Number of peers	.04*	.03	−04*	−05
Number of older peers	−.01	−.05	−01	−02
Drinking Models				
Parental drinking	.10*	.05	01	01
School peers drinking				
Friends drinking	−.23*	−.19*	−22*	−16*
Attitudes				
Social effects	−.12*	−.19*	−18*	−19*
Status reasons	.00	−.03	06*	−04
Personal effects	.01	−.03	01	02
Conforming reasons	.03*	.09	01	03
Behaviors				
Academic grades	−.05*	−.03	−.09*	01
Religiosity	.03*	.07	02*	06
Amount of spending money	−.07*	−10*	−05*	−04
Extent of deviant behavior	−.14*	−13*	−16*	−18*
Marijuana frequency	−.12	−18*	−12*	−15*

lowing variables were significantly related to the amount of consumption among nonblack students: social class, number of peers, status reasons, academic grades, religiosity, and amount of spending money.

An examination of the beta coefficients for alcohol quantity in Table 7-4 reveals a pattern similar to that of drinking frequency. Among black students, however, grade in school (age) predicts amount of consumption but not the frequency of consumption.

With regard to both samples of students, the regression analyses would suggest that the factors associated with the use of alcohol are similar for both black and nonblack students alike.

In light of the similarity of predictor variables within both samples of students, comparisons between both black and nonblack abstainers may reveal factors associated with the later onset of drinking among black students. Table 7-1 summarizes the results of statistical comparisons between the two ethnic/racial groups within each drinker status group. For both abstainers and drinkers, there were significant differences with respect to demographic factors associated with socioeconomic status. It was noted earlier, however, that these variables did not significantly differentiate black abstainers from black drinkers. The results may be interpreted as reflecting more persuasive social class differences between blacks and nonblacks in general. Aside from socioeconomic status, one would expect that black and nonblack abstainers would not differ with regard to the alcohol-related variables. This is true for the most part, but some exceptions can be noted. Among abstainers, nonblack students reported higher proportions of school peers to be drinkers.

A second factor significantly differentiating these two groups relates to the importance of the personal effects of alcohol. Black abstainers, compared to nonblack abstainers, viewed the personal effects of drinking as more important reasons for drinking. Since both groups are nondrinkers, this variable may reflect basic differences in the perception of alcohol between these two groups of students.

In order to assess the overall contributions of these variables while controlling for the effects of demographic differences, a discriminant function analysis was conducted with the two groups of abstinent students. The canonical correlation was .19 (p .001) and the highest standardized coefficients were school peer drinking (-.61) and personal effects (.58). Next in magnitude of contribution were grade in school (.31), socioeconomic status (-.31), and academic grades (.36). These findings indicate that both environmental exposure to drinking models and attitudes regarding the use of alcohol distinguish nonblack and black abstinent students.

SUMMARY AND CONCLUSIONS

The overall objective of this study was to identify factors which relate to the use of alcohol among black and nonblack students and which might serve to explain the lower prevalence of drinking among black students.

Black students were shown to differ from nonblack students with respect to both demographic variables associated with social class and variables associated with exposure to and involvement with alcohol. Multivariate analyses, controlling for the effects of demographic status, yielded several predictors of the frequency and quantity of alcohol consumption. Among the major predictors of alcohol use were exposure to friends as drinking models, attitudes emphasizing the importance of social effects of alcohol, ease of access to alcohol, and behavior patterns of social transgressions and illicit drug use. While degree of religiosity and attainment of good school grades were inversely related to frequent and heavier use of alcohol among nonblack students, they were not related to patterns of alcohol use by black students. For the most part, however, there were more similarities than differences in the predictors of alcohol use among black and nonblack students. These findings suggest that environmental factors associated with the use of alcohol are similar for black and nonblack students.

While the overall use of alcohol is lower among black students, the onset of drinking is grade-related but later in onset relative to nonblack drinkers. Despite the fact that the same predictors of drinking are common to both black and nonblack students, there is need to identify environmental factors which delay exposure to a more extensive network of peer drinking models and access to alcohol.

Comparisons between black and nonblack abstainers revealed that black abstainers reported lower proportions of school peers to be drinkers. This differential exposure to drinking models between black and nonblack abstainers may be implicated in the delay of onset of drinking among black students.

A second factor which may be implicated in the delay of onset of drinking among black students related to differences in the perception of alcohol between blacks and nonblacks. Black abstainers, compared to nonblacks, viewed the personal effects of drinking as more important reasons for drinking. These reasons stress the use of alcohol as a coping mechanism to deal with personal stress and problems.

Future studies need to address the status of these variables with regard to their implications in delaying the onset of drinking among black students.

REFERENCES

Bachman, J. G., Johnston, L. D., and O'Malley, P. M. Smoking, drinking, and drug use among American high school students: Correlates and trends, 1975-1979. *American Journal of Public Health, 71*, 59-69, 1981.

Blane, H. T., and Hewitt, L. E. Alcohol and youth: An analysis of the literature 1960-75. Report No. PB-268-698. Springfield, VA: *U.S. National Technical Information Service,* 1977.

Bourne, P., and Light, E. Alcohol problems in blacks and women. In J. H. Mendelson and N. K. Mello (Eds.), *The diagnosis and treatment of alcoholism.* New York: McGraw-Hill, pp. 83-124, 1979.

Cockerham, W. C. Drinking patterns of institutionalized and noninstitutionalized Wyoming youth. *Journal of Studies on Alcohol, 36,* 993-995, 1975.

Donovan, J., and Jessor, R. Adolescent problem drinking: Psychosocial correlates in a national sample study. *Journal of Studies on Alcohol, 39,* 1506-1524, 1978.

Fishburne, P. M., Abelson, H. I., and Cisin, I. National survey on drug abuse: Main findings: 1979 (Contract No. 271-78-3508). Rockville, MD: *National Institute on Drug Abuse,* 1979.

Harford, T. C., Lowman, C., and Kaelber, C. T. Current prevalence of alcohol use among white and black adolescents. Paper presented at the National Council on Alcoholism Conference, Washington, D.C., April, 1982.

Harper, F. *Alcohol abuse and Black America.* Alexandria, Va.: Douglas Publishers, 1976.

Herd, D. Migration, cultural transformation and the rise of black cirrhosis. Paper presented at the Alcohol Epidemiology Section, International Council on Alcohol and Addictions, Padova, Italy, June 1983.

Jessor, R., and Jessor, S. L. *Problem behavior and psychosocial development: A longitudinal study of youth.* New York: Academic Press, 1977.

Jessor, R., Chase, J. A., and Donovan, J. E. Psychosocial correlates of marijuana use and problem drinking in a national sample of adolescents. *American Journal of Public Health, 70,* 604-613, 1980.

MacKay, J. R., Phillips, D. L., and Bryce, F. O. Drinking behavior among teenagers: A comparison of institutionalized and noninstitutionalized youth. *Journal of Health and Social Behavior, 8*, 46-54, 1967.

Rachal, J. V., Guess, L. L., Hubbard, R. L., Maisto, S. A., Cavanaugh, E. R., Waddell, R., and Benrud, C. D. Adolescent drinking behavior. Volume 1: The extent and nature of adolescent alcohol and drug use: The 1974 and 1978 national sample studies. Research Triangle Park, NC: Research Triangle Institute, 1980.

Rachal, J. V., Williams, J. R., Brehm, M. L., Cavanaugh, B., Moore, R. P., and Eckerman, W. C. A national study of adolescent drinking behavior, attitudes, and correlates. Report No. PB-246-002; NIAAA/NCALI-75/27. Springfield, Va.: *U.S. National Technical Information Service*, 1975.

Rohrbaugh, J., and Jessor, R. Religiosity in youth: A personal control against deviant behavior. *Journal of Personality, 43*, 136-155, 1975.

U.S. Bureau of the Census. School enrollment — Social and economic characteristics of students: October 1980 (Advance Report). Current Population Reports Series P-20, No. 362. Washington, D.C. U.S. Department of Commerce, May, 1981.

Chapter 8

APPROACHING THE PROBLEM

NATIONAL INSTITUTE ON ALCOHOL ABUSE AND ALCOHOLISM

NATIONAL CLEARINGHOUSE FOR ALCOHOL INFORMATION

THE PURPOSE of this chapter is to help black youth develop positive attitudes and behaviors around alcohol use. After reading this, you will:

- Understand what alcohol abuse prevention is
- Be able to list at least four reasons why some black youth try alcohol
- Know what a prevention strategy is
- Understand the difference between alcohol-specific and nonspecific strategies
- Be aware of recommendations from black experts/prevention planners regarding the planning of culturally specific alcohol programs for black youth
- Be able to list nine alcohol prevention strategies that can help youth develop more positive attitudes and behaviors about alcohol use

OVERVIEW

Approaching the problem of alcohol abuse among black youth begins with some of the same elements that apply to youth in other ethnic groups. The difference, however, is in certain issues that affect black people in general, such as high unemployment, and have a significant impact on youth. Also, unique to blacks is a rich cultural history, with roots in Africa, an important consideration in helping youth build self-pride so essential to fostering positive drinking behaviors. In addition to discussing the role of black culture, this chapter also explains prevention theory and current ideas on why young people choose to drink, including the influence of value systems, role models, and the media. Finally, nine prevention strategies suitable for use with black adolescents are described. These activities range from exploring black history to producing alcohol-related television shows and developing problem solving skills.

WHAT IS PREVENTION?

To prevent something is to keep it from happening. As it is used in this book, prevention refers to taking actions that will change harmful drinking practices. Such actions may be taken by the individual, as well as by the community as a whole. The purpose of prevention, then, is to increase the likelihood that individuals who do drink will develop drinking behaviors that are personally and socially healthy. Appropriate drinking and appropriate situational abstinence can be taught through activities that provide youth the opportunity to:

- Enhance self-esteem
- Develop a sense of purpose
- Promote respect for self and others
- Promote individual dignity
- Develop personal and social skills necessary for effective functioning in society
- Avoid alcohol-related problems

The goal, then, is to affect youth by developing healthy attitudes that will in turn change behavior. Of equal importance is information on alcohol, its effects, and the role it plays in the life of an individual and in the individual's community. These two components together can aid youth in making decisions about alcohol use. Since drinking really is a normal experience of life, it should not be viewed as deviant behavior; offering information from a moralistic point of view is not likely to produce healthy drinking attitudes.

Alcohol abuse prevention is concerned with providing alcohol information to a wide variety of groups and individuals, including those who may not be experiencing any alcohol-related problems at the moment. Young people who do not habitually abuse alcohol are among this target group. Unfortunately, there are other persons, some of them adolescents, who may be involved with alcohol to a greater degree. They may exhibit:

- *Nonsevere drinking problems* that interfere with a person's expected or chosen role, but do not prevent that person from carrying out the basic functions of life. Examples include sleeping through classes the morning after a drinking party, family friction about a teenager's drinking habits, tardiness, or lack of concentration on the job.
- *Severe drinking problems* that hinder the person from carrying out the basic functions of his/her role. Examples include the inability to attend school, regularly hold down a job, or sustain meaningful relationships with peers, as a result of heavy drinking or dependence on alcohol.

All these groups — those with no problems, those with nonsevere problems, and those with severe problems — are potential targets for alcohol abuse prevention efforts. Deciding on an appropriate way to reach these groups calls for some basic information on why young people drink and in particular, what special forces encourage drinking among black adolescents.

UNDERSTANDING DRINKING BEHAVIOR

The motivations for drinking by young people are not fully understood. Experts offer various explanations such as peer pressure and a youth's need to make independent decisions about one's life, including alcohol.

What forces and influences are operating that encourage an adolescent to value drinking as a desirable behavior? Some possible explanations include:

- The youth's value system
- The influence of role models
- The influence of the media
- Other factors such as unemployment and easy access to liquor

Value Systems

One's value system may be an influence. A value system, the sum of forces and influences that shape a person's life, are important to understand when planning a program. Part of that value system is the image that drinking creates for some youth.

A value system is composed of standards developed as a result of information acquired during childhood and adult life. Youth can accept, reject, add to, or subtract from these standards. Role models are the key to the development of these standards. People as well as sets of events give youth examples to emulate. These examples prove to be a positive or negative influence on the final character and behavior of young people. Helping youth build positive value systems is a part of building self-pride in the individual as a member of a distinct cultural group.

Role Models

Current research suggests that teenage drinking is one of many acts that marks the transition to adulthood. Drinking by youth therefore may be a learned and predictable aspect of behavior in a drinking society (Jessor and Jessor, 1975). If this theory is correct, then we must consider reasons for youth's drinking to be similar to those for adults. These include: (1) to relax and have fun, (2) as part of a social function (something to do), (3) to be part of the crowd and therefore accepted by peers, (4) to release inhibitions, and (5) to cope with anxiety, pressure, or conflict (Blane and Hewitt, 1977).

Although research information on alcohol and blacks is limited, black alcohol experts generally agree that as black youths mature, they need positive adult role models. Models come from many sources — the street, the home, the church, schools, social service agencies, the media, and a variety of other sources. Since some of these are negative, especially those on TV and other communication channels, youth must be exposed to positive role models for counterbalance.

The Media

Media messages in magazines, on billboards, and on TV associate alcohol with maturity, glamour, and sophistication. Liquor advertisers in 1975 spent $1,846,910 for 136.91 pages of advertising in *Ebony Magazine* to promote the use of various beers, wines, and liquors by the black consumer. The intent of these expensive ad campaigns is to create a desire for liquor. Slick looking black models are used in ads that convey an image of success and "having made it." These ads play on the unconscious desires of people, black youth in particular, to be somebody. These ads create the illusion that liquor will bring strength, success, glamour, wealth, and sexual conquest.

The TV industry also does its part to contribute to the image that alcohol is a necessity of life. In prime time television entertainment programs, drunkenness is often portrayed as humorous. The good-natured drunk provokes laughter through slow and incoherent speech and disoriented behavior. These are a few of the subtle messages that television offers to youth. The images portrayed say that alcohol use is okay — an accepted part of the American way of life.

According to an article by John Dillin of the *Christian Science Monitor*, alcoholic drinks are featured in 80 percent of TV network prime-time shows. In some cases as often as every 8 minutes, alcoholic beverages are drunk, poured, shown on the screen in various other ways, or mentioned by performers. In the programs that depict real life situations, such as soap operas, characters turn to alcohol to relieve the stress and personal conflicts they may be experiencing as a part of the plot. Alcohol is portrayed as a problem solver.

Other Influences

In addition to the media, other influences significantly affect how black youth see themselves. These influences — high unemployment, abundance of liquor stores in black neighborhoods, the constant "drunk" on the corner — daily reinforce negative self-images and the condition of black oppression in the United States.

Unemployment is the number one problem adults cite as a black community priority. Alcohol and drug abuse in black lower-income communities is a coping response to unemployment, poverty, and all of the accompanying social and economic derivatives. Black youth are forced into idleness by the lack of jobs available to them, thereby, "hanging out on corners" and drinking or abusing drugs becomes "something to do." Dr. Benjamin Whitten, Vocational Educational Director, Baltimore City Schools (1976), reveals that: "Youth who graduate from high school are eager to find jobs and work at improving their marketable skills. However, constant disappointments created by a lack of job opportunities over a period of two or three years cause black youth to develop an unemployed lifestyle. They become accustomed to not working and after some months or years, stop looking for work." If Dr. Whitten's observations are correct, it is probably during this period of developing an unemployed lifestyle that youth between the ages of 17 and 22 develop their pattern of heavy drinking.

Liquor is easily obtainable, a factor contributing to youthful alcohol abuse. Impact studies indicate that in low-income black communities the liquor outlets are more prevalent than in any other places throughout most urban areas.

A frequent phenomenon of lower-income black neighborhoods that may produce a negative self-image is the constancy of the "drunk" in the gutter, on the corner, or sleeping in a doorway. Youngsters on their way to elementary school daily confront the neighborhood "drunk." The "drunk" is so much a part of the fabric of the low-income neighborhood that the individual becomes almost invisible to those who live there. Existence of this person, however, does have an affect on neighborhood youngsters. In low-income areas, the "drunk" is the alternative model to abstinence. Further, the community often becomes insensitive to this daily figure because there are other priorities — economic survival.

A recent study of adolescents that included a small sample of black youth showed that drinking among these adolescents was often associated with low self-esteem, a sense of powerlessness, poor interpersonal and social skills, poor academic or vocational performance, negative peer pressure, and poor family relationships (Nowliss, 1979). The social and economic conditions that blacks experience in America can also be offered as an explanation for using and/or abusing alcohol. Intense feelings of oppression often lead to a search for escape through whatever means are available. Sometimes that escape is through alcohol.

Youth Alcohol Abuse: A Serious Problem

Alcohol abuse by youth is a serious problem in the United States. It is estimated that 3.3 million youth are problem drinkers and, therefore, encounter alcohol-related problems. Youth, themselves, define these problems as getting into trouble with teachers or principals and getting into difficulties with friends. Youth and young adults are often agents as well as victims of the estimated 46,000 motor vehicle fatalities that are alcohol-related.

In a national study of black men under 20 years of age, 25 percent of those committing crimes against property had been drinking, and 30 percent of those committing crimes against persons had been drinking (Roizen, 1979). More research studies are needed on the drinking patterns of black youth, particularly those that are designed and directed by black researchers. Lack of data discourages us from drawing any concrete conclusions and developing suitable programing. Efforts to help black youth, however, cannot wait for the results of further studies. It is essential to begin now and take action to change destructive drinking behaviors.

CHANGING DRINKING BEHAVIOR

Many successful youth prevention programs have developed prevention strategies or ways to change the behavior and attitudes necessary to lessen the incidence of alcohol-related problems. Such strategies attempt to help youth to see beyond their present situation and help them to focus on the broader issues of life and the future.

Prevention Strategies

A strategy is an action, set of actions or activities, that is used to reach a specific goal. Alcohol prevention strategies are actions taken to keep harmful drinking behaviors from occurring.

Traditionally, two kinds of prevention strategies have been employed at the community level: alcohol-specific strategies and nonspecific strategies. Although neither approach alone has definitely proven successful, it does appear that programs that combine both specific and nonspecific strategies have the greatest likelihood of affecting drinking behavior.

It should be noted here that not all the material offered in the remainder of this chapter is culturally-specific; rather, it is based on information drawn from long-established prevention efforts geared to youth in general. Because these strategies have been successful, planners of black youth prevention programs are advised to look at suggested strategies and adapt them for use with their particular target groups.

Alcohol-specific Strategies

Alcohol-specific strategies deal directly with alcohol or drinking to influence what people drink, how much, how often, when, why, where, or even the way they drink (sipping vs. gulping, for example). The following examples are specific strategies that might be used to minimize alcohol abuse:

- Providing alcohol education in the schools
- Sponsoring alcohol education programs using peers
- Promoting of peer social groups and attitudes that oppose drunkenness, driving when drinking, and other dangerous behavior
- Encouraging of responsible role modeling by parents and others who drink
- Conducting alcohol-related film festivals/symposia/conferences
- Examining of alcohol-related laws/legislation to see how potential modification might decrease alcohol-related problems
- Providing of substitute environments for youthful experimentation with alcohol, such as teen activities
- Training bartenders to expand their helping role as listeners and referral sources for all types of problems
- Developing programs designed to keep intoxicated persons from driving
- Developing public awareness campaigns to limit the numbers of alcohol ads and billboards in the community
- Supporting zoning restrictions to remove bars and taverns from the proximity of schools and churches or to lower the density in the community
- Organizing community efforts to counter media glamorization of alcohol consumption

Particularly in the black community, strategies must directly counteract negative influences, such as numerous alcohol ads, the incidence of taverns, and bars adjacent to schools and churches, and the availability of alcohol in grocery stores (Dawkins, 1979). All alcohol-specific strategies call for clear and consise information on the debilitating effects that alcohol use/abuse has on the stability of the individual and the community. Such information is needed for planning youth programs, training bartenders as helpers, or holding alcohol-related film festivals or conferences. The content of the information should include the physical and psychological aspects of alcohol; common myths and misconceptions about alcohol; signs of alcohol abuse and how to recognize the signs in self and in others. The progressive stages leading to alcoholism, as well as ways to get help when needed, should also be included.

To assure that youth are able to relate to the information, it should be written in language they can easily understand. Black heritage, culture, and the history of alcohol use and abuse among blacks as a whole, and in the particular community, are also important. Information on the availability of and accessibility to alcohol locally is also needed for planning ways to positively influence youthful drinking.

Nonalcohol-specific Strategies

Nonalcohol-specific strategies attempt to influence drinking patterns and drinking behavior indirectly. They do not deal directly with alcohol, but rather with the broader aspects of living. Nonspecific strategies include offering alternatives to drinking and attempting to facilitate interpersonal relations. Strategies that are non-alcohol-specific include:

- Values clarification and related activities to improve decision-making ability by young people
- Assertiveness training
- Projects aimed at developing coping skills
- Projects that teach alternative methods of relaxing, for example sports/recreation, TM, yoga
- Projects aimed at increasing creative skills and learning to communicate and deal more effectively with others

- Job-finding skills
- Job-training skills
- Provision of comfortable settings for youth to interact with adults on a nonjudgmental basis
- Development of peer counselor programs to assist young people with personal problems
- Improvement of economic, cultural, and other qualities of life in the community
- Increase in opportunities for recreation and other alternatives to drinking
- Programs to enhance the skills youth already have
- Programs to make the educational system more responsive to student needs
- Increase in opportunities for social interaction between youth where alcohol is not involved

Regardless of what strategies are chosen, two important factors should be kept in mind:

Involvement of youth is crucial in all stages of program planning, implementation, and evaluation. Serious input by young people not only lends credibility to a program, but will also contribute fresh thinking and creativity.

Prevention strategies should be designed to influence as much of the total environment as possible. Because alcohol use and abuse are intertwined with so many aspects of life (home, school, media, advertising, law, the economy, and the community), any strategy limited to a single element, such as home or school, can achieve only limited objectives. The most meaningful strategy is one that promotes responsible behavior around the use or nonuse of alcohol among the young and reduces the personal and social damage associated with inappropriate usage.

Alcoholism and Its Place in
Youth Prevention Projects

In addition to issues of specific versus nonspecific strategies, as appropriate for use in youth alcohol prevention programs, experts who design programs advise that emphasis on alcoholism and medical or physical symptoms is not productive. Alcoholism, as it is used

here, refers to recurring drinking problems severe enough to interfere with daily living.

At the 1976 Forum of the National Council on Alcoholism Workshop on Alcohol and Youth, Dr. Don Cahalan suggested that, for
teenagers, problems with alcohol are usually related to events, such
as accidents and encounters with the law, rather than to physical
conditions such as a deteriorating liver condition caused by excessive
drinking. He urged those working with young people to pay more
attention to the specific drinking problem or disruptive behavior
than to predictors of alcoholism or medical symptoms. Actually focusing on drinking behavior initially may be detrimental because alcohol is not part of the youth agenda. Youth, for the most part, are
concerned about the problems of growing up, parents, siblings, and
peers.

Dr. Robert Strauss, College of Medicine, University of Ken-
tucky, in *Alcohol and Society* (1973), distinguished between problem
drinkers responding to needs within themselves and those responding to needs that stem from the social and cultural setting in which
they drink. He suggested that most young problem drinkers fall into
the latter category and noted that as long as the pressures to drink
"too much" are outside the individual, strategies for prevention that
stress alcoholism are not useful.

The Boys Harbor Alcohol Education Program, an alcohol education program serving minority youth in New York City, concludes
that the principal problem for youngsters between the ages of 15 and
24 is not alcoholism nor severe alcohol involvment, but the negative
consequences of intoxication (NCALI, 1977).

Dr. Gail Milgram, Rutgers Center for Alcohol Studies, stressed
that, in a program that deals with drinking in the broader context,
young people who are not having problems will be exposed to information that is relevant to them and young people who are having
problems will be more easily able to identify their problem behavior
without having to accept a label of alcoholism.

Putting Prevention to Work for Black Youth

So far, this chapter has discussed the concept of prevention; understanding drinking behavior in terms of value systems, role

models, and other influences; and changing drinking behavior through alcohol specific and nonspecific strategies. The remaining pages present strategies that can be used to assist black youth in making decisions about alcohol.

PROGRAMMING STRATEGIES FOR BLACK YOUTH

As noted earlier, little formal research has been done on alcohol prevention programs for black youth. However, a wide range of recommendations and ideas on designing programs have come from persons who have worked with youth, and others with backgrounds in black history and social problems and issues affecting blacks today.

Ron Karenga, in cooperation with the Institute for Positive Education, has developed a black values system approach that can be useful as a foundation for a black alcohol prevention program. The principles may be used in a number of ways in an alcohol prevention education program for black youth. It may be adapted to meet special needs. It is a beginning, a theoretical framework, and a system to which blacks can quickly relate. It is culturally specific and youth as well as community-oriented.

- *Umoja (unity)*: to strive for and maintain unity in the family, community, nation, and race.
- *Kujichajulia (self-determination)*: To define ourselves, name ourselves, and speak for ourselves instead of being defined and spoken for by others.
- *Ujima (collective work and responsibility)*: To build and maintain our community together and to make our brothers' and sisters' problems our problems and to solve them together.
- *Ujama (cooperative economics)*: To build and own stores, shops, and other businesses, and to profit together from them.
- *Nea (purpose)*: To make as our collective vocation the building and developing of our community in order to restore our people to their traditional greatness.
- *Kuumba (creativity)*: To do always as much as we can, in the way we can, in order to leave our community more beautiful and beneficial than when we inherited it.

- *Imani (faith)*: To believe in our parents, our teachers, our leaders, our people, and ourselves, and the righteousness and victory of our struggle.

Other experts have offered the following advice:

- *Importance of Black History/Culture*. Programs achieving the greatest success have adapted a culturally specific, alcohol-specific education model that focuses on the individual and his/her environment. Black history, self-awareness, and values are all integrated into a broader framework focused on a citizen in a multicultural pluralistic society. Cultural identity is an important aspect of the alcohol education program. There is and there should be sensitivity toward the language and terminology used to connote a racial or cultural heritage, religion, or color.

- *Building Positive Self-Concepts*. An alcohol education program for black youth must implement strategies that will provide opportunities for these youngsters to discard negativism. True, many of them have been hardened by the reality of their life-styles, but it is possible to help them see beyond the present and set positive goals for the future. What is important is changing their attitudes about themselves and getting them involved in meaningful activities.

- *Emphasis on Survival Skills*. The process of the program must teach survival skills such as problem solving, decision-making, and valuing. It is important to point out to black youth that everyone has problems. There are problems connected with jobs, school, family, and with living in general. When the problems are erased, living does not exist. Living is problem-solving. The issue is not how many or how big the problem is, but learning how to find solutions.

- *Sensitivity to the Special Issues of Adolescence*. Prevention programers should be in touch with some of the lessons learned in the youth movement. For example: What are the most important issues in the lives of young people? Whom do they visualize as their friends? Whom do they see as their enemies? All of these questions should be answered before starting a program.

- *Providing a Balance of Specific and Nonspecific Strategies*. Youth need knowledge about the positive and negative aspects of alcohol as well as specialized skills for making choices about drinking and the other important issues affecting them. Specific alcohol strategies, such as alcohol education information, and nonspecific strategies, such as decision-making skills, are ways to accomplish this.

How program planners can take the topics discussed above and put prevention to work in programs for black youth is outlined in the following pages. Each prevention strategy begins with background on why it is important and is followed by a description of the specific activity.

Strategy 1: Cultural Approach

Background.

What purpose does culture serve in an alcohol prevention program? Ever wonder why individuals drink the way they do? Or why some people don't drink? Why Abdul Sabazz or Reverend Johnson emphatically denounce alcohol? How many groups drink only at certain times, for example dinnertime, weddings, funerals, Christmas, or bar mitzvahs?

Much of what people do is influenced by culture. This is supported by many anthropological studies such as: Vernon J. Dixon's explanation of cultural world views; Edward Sapir's study of the relationship between language and culture; Ruth Benedict's studies of culture and personality; and Frederic Harper's discussion of alcoholism and the black community. This research shows that cultural factors influence, not only language and personality, but also whether, · how much, and why a person drinks. Such evidence make a firm case for the development of culturally-specific alcohol prevention programs. An understanding of the uniqueness of black culture is necessary if effective cultural-specific prevention efforts are to make an impact on black adolescents and their communities.

Activity.

The cultural approach to alcohol prevention stresses black heritage and a sense of pride in one's self. Projects of this nature should:

- Provide factual information about the country from which one's parents or ancestors came
- Provide for identification with a civilization or historical epoch

during which one's family and ancestors were free of cultural domination by conquest or exploitation

- Use terms that arise out of people's pride in their heritage or in their present struggle for justice
- Use terms that allow the individual to transcend a period of history when the dominant society used polite language, such as colored, or similar terms
- Use peer-respected terminology, recognized slang or jargon
- Provide factual information that eliminates stereotypical images

One approach to exploring black history is to form a cultural study group. A product of the "black pride" movement of the 1960s, cultural groups still have relevance in providing black youth with a sense of pride, heritage, and positive role models. Activities that focus on Afro-American or African history, including language, power structures, dance, music, art, family traditions, and other cultural forms, help create a sense of identity, pride, and personal integrity.

While learning about black history, black youngsters can also build skills in conducting historical and anthropological research in local libraries or universities. There are a number of alcohol-related topics that can be included in this cultural exploration.

Following is a beginning list:

- How did the use of alcohol change in America during the years 1600-1980?
- How was alcohol use encouraged/discouraged among blacks during the years 1600-1980?
- What elements of appeal are used in liquor advertisements in the black community?
- Are there two sets of social standards in regard to alcohol use/alcoholism treatment, one for men and another for women?
- What associations are there between alcohol use and various religious groups?

Strategy 2: Other Cultures

Background.

Studying other cultures provides youth an opportunity to gain new knowledge to help them establish their own ground rules for alcohol use. Other cultures, such as the Judiac and fundamentalist

Christian, have developed traditions of alcohol use that differ from blacks. These and selected others historically have had low consumption rates. Information of this nature may stimulate discussions on transferring certain aspects of these cultures to black communities.

Activity.

The youth participating in an alcohol prevention program can carry out library research to investigate these cultures, or program staff can research the topic and design arts and crafts projects or conduct discussion groups. The following suggestions may help you to begin planning in this direction:

- Determine which mood-changing chemicals are legitimate within the black community; as background material, find information on the following cultural practices:
  - Orthodox Jews allow wine only.
  - Orthodox Muslims allow no mood-changing chemicals.
  - Many fundamentalist Christians allow no mood-changing chemicals.
  - American Indians allow peyote, mescaline, psilocybine, and alcohol (i.e., beer).
  - Lo Bir Africans drink only beer.
- Establish rules on how legitimate chemicals should be used:
  - When is legitimate use permitted?
  - Where is legitimate use permitted?
  - What occasions are legitimate for use?
  - What behavior is legitimate while using these chemicals?
- Establish clear methods of communicating the rules, for example, through family, church, black media, and schools.
- Determine community ownership by establishing clear accountability systems within the black community and by identifying consequences of ignoring/disobeying established rules (Bell, 1979).

Strategy 3: Life Skills/Survival Skills

Background.

Because black youth are often confined to their communities, they lack knowledge of and exposure to the majority community, often making any contact frustrating, intimidating, or frightening. Lower-income youth, however, do have a cadre of skills which they developed through necessity. Many of these youngsters assumed adult responsibilities when they were very young. Some have complete charge of younger brothers and sisters, do economical grocery shopping with food stamps, manage households while their mother works or is absent from the home. Many youngsters take on this responsibility as early as age six. So, black youth do have a base of knowledge for learning coping and survival skills.

Activity: Neighborhood Awareness.

Life skills can be developed as youths build a better awareness of their neighborhoods and themselves. Ways to do this are:

- Planning field trips to: local goverment offices to learn how municipal services are delivered in their neighborhood; to banks to investigate how savings and checking accounts work; to the consumer protection office to learn about credit laws and rights of consumers
- Conducting shopping expeditions to teach comparison shopping
- Getting youth involved in voter registration drives to make them aware of election processes and their voting rights and duties
- Discussing family budgeting
- Discovering location and services of alcohol treatment facilities

Activity: Problem Solving.

Youth need to first practice a step-by-step problem solving routine for simple nonthreatening problems and then graduate to solving life problems using the same process. Suggested are the following steps:

- Define the problem; think about the problem; identify the essential characteristics of the problem; determine the real problem and any contributing factors
- Establish expectations; ask yourself, "If the problem could be solved, what would be the results? What would be achieved if the problem were solved?

- Collect information; gather facts; get the opinions of others; place all information in the subconscious, letting it rest there awhile
- Gather solutions; collect possible solutions, answers or actions for the problem; the more you have, the broader your alternative possibilities
- Determine a course of action; select one or more of the courses of action that would seem to accomplish the goals or objectives you have established; take action; do not be overcome by the fear of a wrong course of action; if the first selected action fails, choose from a variety of alternatives and try another course of action.

It is possible that the course of action taken will not lead to a solution. Do not be discouraged. There are some problems in life for which there are not solutions. However, the problem can be acted upon, the situation can be altered, conditions managed, and progress achieved. The final step in the problem-solving process requires that one make a decision and choose one or two alternative courses of action that may lead to a sound, rational course of action.

Activity: Decision-making.

A reality of the black experience has been the lack of opportunities for blacks to make decisions for themselves. Consequently, many low-income blacks shy away from decision-making. Black youth, in particular those from low-income neighborhoods, have had little opportunity to become involved with decision-making or policy-making, even on a small scale such as neighborhood or youth councils. They have had little or no involvement in youth leadership groups such as scouts or boys' clubs and girls' clubs. Additionally, American culture has taught children that bad decisions may result in scolding and punishments, so children learn to straddle the fence, or are pressured into going along with the crowd's decision. As a result, when they reach adolescence, decision-making skills are acutely retarded. It is essential that black youth learn how to make decisions, because if they do not, circumstances will determine the situation for them.

One way to begin helping youth with this important life skill is to

use role play to teach decision-making. Within the setting of the prevention program, the activity could be carried out as follows:

- Select a topic for the role play, such as deciding whether or not
  to drink wine with friends before driving a car
- Assign parts for the role play: the youth making the decision,
  several friends trying to persuade the youth to drink, one person to record the pros and cons of drinking before driving
- Allow the dialog among the friends to continue for about 10
  minutes
- Discuss the dialog; the adult leader will facilitate the discussion
  by going over the list of pros and cons; for example, the
  dangers in mixing alcohol with driving, the feeling of being left
  out if one does not drink.

The intent of this discussion is to help youth understand how decisions are made, to allow youth to project themselves into a situation and practice the process of rational decision-making in a
learning and supportive environment. This exercise is also intended
to show youth that it is acceptable to make decisions, find out that
they are not workable, and change them. No course of action is cast
in concrete, nor should it be.

Strategy 4: Community-wide Approach

Background.

Accomplishments by black people in striving for and maintaining
unity in family, community, nation, and race have resulted from collective action. Where youth are concerned, collective action is
needed to promote positive attitudes and behaviors around alcohol.
Working together, the individuals and groups in a community can
do much to help youth.

Activity.

Development of a cultural group norm should be viewed as a social policy strategy aimed first at identifying the alcohol behavior of
concern to the black community; second, correlating the concerns
with defined social change goals; and, third, establishing a scheme
for effective positive change. Essentially, the correlation should act

as a catalyst for development of rules, norms, standards, and an appropriate cultural system of accountability that deals specifically with the use of alcohol in the black community.

The creation of a social group norm for drinking in the American black community is an example of a unifying force or collective action strategy. This strategy can be divided into major and minor activities. For example, a major activity could be an environmental health campaign designed to minimize the number of alcohol billboards, number of visible "hang-out" areas used by drinkers, and number of grocery stores that sell alcohol.

This focus would require developing vehicles for organizing the campaign, i.e., community improvement associations, ad hoc neighborhood clubs, and health promotion groups organized temporarily as a part of existing community institutions such as churches. Information and activities relating to a social group norm can be developed through the use of the main access routes designed by society, i.e., the family, educational, recreational, prevention, treatment, and health maintenance institutions.

In the broad context of the community, the access routes include: schools, churches, intact and ad hoc adult/youth groups, block clubs, recreation programs, PTAs, juvenile justice programs, community health agencies, after-school programs, cultural groups, summer youth programs, community black groups, movie theaters, and other local media. All of these or some can be included in this community-wide policy development on acceptable alcohol use.

Many of these groups who work directly with youth can implement environmental research activities on a much smaller scale. Youth can meet together and describe a healthy environment for their neighborhood. They can be sent out into the community to observe and compare their observations with the projection of how they would like their environment to be. They can then make a list of the changes that have to be made in order to meet their projected healthy environment goal. The activities necessary to effect change can be listed in a plan with a timetable and the other people to be involved. This project can be as simple as posting a "No Loitering" sign or as difficult as having alcohol billboards removed or alcohol sales outlets closed after certain hours or permanently.

Community people must decide the place of alcohol in their environment. They have the power to establish norms. Some activities toward this end may be:

- Identify black heroes at national and local levels that will attract the attention of blacks, win their respect, and address the need for a community social policy on alcohol.
- Develop group sanctions against drunkenness followed by public proclamation by national black groups and their local chapters.
- Develop a community consensus regarding appropriate drinking behavior in the black community by:
    - Encouraging clear, established rules on the use of alcohol (when and where)
    - Providing a method of communicating the established rules
    - Investigating viable alternatives
    - Designing culturally-specific and relevant alternative methods of coping with stress (Bell, 1979).

The ultimate goal of the community approach is to provide black youth with positive role models, accurate information about the history of alcohol and blacks, an appreciation for the environment, and a vehicle for transferring the rules for proper drinking behavior to black youth as part of an alcohol problem prevention campaign.

Strategy 5: Youth Involvement

Backgound.

Many "youth programs" operate for years with problem youth who have been referred by social service and legal agencies. As soon as the assigned time is completed, the youth leave because there is nothing to hold them in the program. However, it has been proven that youth who are involved in the planning and implementation of the program remain long after their court-appointed referrals have expired. Therefore, youth involvement as part of the planning ensures "ownership" and fosters stability in a program. The involvement of youth can be accomplished in a number of ways.

Activity: Peer Counseling.

Well-trained peer counselors can often do more than professional counselors to help a troubled youth. Through specially designed programs, youth are trained to serve as counselors or facilitators. These youth, in turn, help their peers cope with or handle social, emotional, and practical problems. Such youth helpers should have skills in active and empathetic listening, feedback, and reflection techniques. The individuals can help their peers affirm personal capabilities, strengths, talents, and abilities that contribute to the full realization of positive self-image and self-actualization.

Activity: Peer Leadership.

Peer leaders are a small group of young people who are trained in the content area of alcohol, skill areas of the small group process, and facilitation of group discussion. These youth serve to educate their peers by providing alcohol-specific information. Many programs use their peer leaders as outreach workers to speak to schools, youth clubs, and community organizations.

Developing a social network of youth is a significant aspect of prevention activities, because it enables youth to organize themselves and develop into strong leaders. Identifying promising youth leadership, engaging them, and channeling their energies and gifts result in a win/win/win situation for the individual, the prevention program, and the community. Training black youth to be positive peer models and leaders can be a strong component in prevention programs.

Activity: Partners in the Program.

In beginning a youth program, both the planning and implementation process should provide for total youth involvement from membership on steering committees to voting positions on the board of directors. In this way youth will have input into the decisions that directly affect them. Youth should be involved as partners in the planning process for new programs, and already operating programs should include youth as paid workers, volunteers, peer leaders, and board members.

Strategy 6: Parent, School, and Church Involvement

Background.

Making contact with as many facets of the youth's life as possible is a means for reinforcing positive messages about drinking attitudes and behavior. The family, the school, and the church have significant roles to play in the alcohol abuse prevention process.

Activity: Parents.

The formation of black parent advisory groups can be an effective way to lobby boards of education to include culturally specific prevention models in school health curricula. Parents should also be included in planning groups with youth to determine future directions for youth programs. Parents can be helpful as volunteers to programs and as chaperones for special group activities. The experience of parents and youth working and planning together encourages more involvement at home. Children tend to talk more freely with their parents, and parents learn parenting skills and a way of influencing the quality of family life.

Activity: School.

Prevention programs often have maximum impact when offered by agencies that can provide educational supports to youth, including tutoring, counseling, and assistance in getting into or preparing for college. Whenever possible, the education support efforts should be connected with schools. Contacting PTAs and school curriculum committees is a means for coordinating the efforts of the prevention program with existing school health education projects. Those projects that do not include alcohol information may be made aware of the community prevention effort as an available resource.

Activity: Church.

The church is becoming more concerned about alcohol use and abuse among its congregation and among youth in particular. Alcohol information efforts for churches may focus on alcohol use by different age groups with special emphasis on youth. All approaches directed to church groups, Sunday schools, and ministers should be educative, with information simply stated and applicable strategies clearly listed. Suggestions include sending out flyers that give information and scientific data, as well as statistics on alcohol-related problems that can be used for a Sunday Gospel. When enlisting the help of ministers, it is necessary to take a commonsense approach that emphasizes the family and alcohol problems.

Strategy 7: The Media Approach

Background.

The media — radio, TV, magazines, billboards, tape shows — can be used as a vehicle for prevention messages. Since the media is used to promote alcohol use, its techniques can be studied and adapted to promote alcohol prevention.

Activity.

Essential to this activity is basic knowledge about alcohol and its use by the media. Of particular interest are investigations of why blacks are shown sipping drinks in glamorous situations and what impact this has on young people in deciding to drink. Local people, such as professors or skillful students from communication and media departments of colleges and universities, can be tapped for technical assistance. Local television and radio stations may also be contacted for assistance on the project.

After the alcohol information and media information have been covered, the youth in the program should plan a media project of their own. This may include posters, radio spots, TV spots, 8 mm films, or slide-tape shows. Following careful planning around the available resources, the project can then be produced and presented before parents, classrooms, and other groups of youngsters.

Magazine advertising plays a major role in influencing alcohol consumption among blacks. To develop awareness of advertising as a form of persuasion, program participants may be assigned the task of conducting a content analysis of two national black magazines to count the number of liquor ads. Next have them analyze the actual messages. What are the promised rewards? How realistic are they? Learning about the persuasive power of advertising can also be accomplished through looking at hit record campaigns conducted to popularize a new record. The record campaign is a good attention-getter because it is a familiar part of adolescent life.

An additional assignment on this same topic calls for the counting of billboards in a certain area and identifying the number specifically advertising liquor. The percent of liquor advertisments can be calculated from this. A variation of this assignment is to count liquor billboard advertisements in white or Hispanic neighborhoods and compare the count to billboard advertisements in black neighborhoods.

All of these assignments will involve youth with their community in mini-research projects to analyze the degree to which they and society as a whole are subtly programmed by the constancy of the same message — liquor will do great things for you.

Strategy 8: Legal/Legislative Approach

Background.

As both a community prevention strategy and a developmental activity for youth, legal/legislative activities present opportunities to look at the controls that determine how liquor is sold. Understanding of the control system is a first step toward making that system more responsive to black neighborhood problems associated with alcohol.

Activity.

By joining forces, youths enrolled in prevention programs and adult community groups can work together to reduce the number and concentration of liquor stores and bars in black communities by pressing local governments to conduct environmental impact studies, by polling community opinions on numbers and locations of liquor outlets in black neighborhoods, and by voicing opposition to the proposed opening of new package stores or bars by contacting members of the local zoning boards, or State ABC agencies, depending on the structure of State authority.

Legislative activities can include observing relevant committees at work in the local legislature or studying the procedures for placing a referendum on the ballot and campaigning for its passage. Library or government agency research can be conducted to find out the amount of revenue collected by the city from liquor taxes, liquor licenses, and other liquor-related activities such as entertainment taxes. If available, taxes collected in white middle-class neighborhoods can be compared to taxes collected in black neighborhoods. The purpose of investigating liquor taxes is to explain taxation in general and enable youth to learn about consumption patterns in their own community. An additional activity dealing with the legal/legislative area is to research zoning laws, practices, and licensing procedures for the sale of liquor. This builds an understanding of how local and state laws operate and the role that liquor plays in the legal system.

Strategy 9: Sports, Arts and Crafts, and Music

Background.

With a view toward keeping youth interested in the program, it is important to have a variety of activities to offer, discouraging the "not that again" complaints. Sports, arts and crafts, and music offer opportunities to keep the approach fresh and exciting.

Activity: Sports.

Sports activities are a staple in many black youth programs because they provide an excellent opportunity to deal with team effort as cooperation rather than as cut-throat competition. Sports activities should be structured by prevention staff with input from youth. For school or city league play, it is important that there be black participation and representation in planning and developing of all activities.

Training for sports and athletic skill development provides many opportunities for coaches and teams to discuss good health principles and practices. Appropriate topics include the effects of alcohol on the body under stress in athletic competition, the physiological aspects of alcohol abuse, and the reasons why certain players do not use alcohol.

Activity: Arts and Crafts.

Arts and crafts can be a useful vehicle for creative expression around alcohol prevention. Youths who have reading problems may have a special interest in this kind of activity. All of the crafts should have an alcohol-related message. Whatever crafts are selected, a professional in that particular field should be tapped to teach the skill. Parents can also be used as volunteer consultants on arts and crafts projects. Skills, such as silk screening, puppet making, playwriting and scenic production, macrame, diorama construction, and photography, can be taught and used by youngsters to construct projects with alcohol-related messages.

Activity: Music.

Music, too, can be used as a medium to convey messages about alcohol to youth and adults via projects in classes and youth programs. Youth tend to be very oriented toward popular music. Songs and "ditties" can be composed by youth to convey alcohol abuse prevention messages.

SUMMARY

Because drinking is part of American society and black culture as well, youth alcohol prevention efforts should focus on teaching responsible decision-making about alcohol use. An understanding of why youth drink, the influences of role models and value systems, and the significance of black culture are important considerations when designing behavioral change programs. Where feasible, planners should incorporate culturally-specific strategies and activities into their program plans, consulting with similar ongoing black community efforts for assistance. Such efforts may include abstinence, an alternative that may be appropriate for some youngsters. Additionally, traditional prevention strategies that have successfully served other youth populations can be adapted and made relevant to black youngsters, provided the new program is philosophically committed to recognizing the importance of cultural differences. At issue in the planning process also is an understanding of the potentially broad target audience involved, including (1) those youngsters who have never tried alcohol, (2) those with nonsevere drinking problems, and (3) those with severe drinking problems. All three groups require alcohol education information tailored to their special needs in programs that involve their participation and that help build futures that are free of destructive drinking behaviors.

REFERENCES

Bell, P. Paper presented to Colorado Black Alcoholism Task Force. Spring, 1979.

Blane, H.T., and Hewitt, L.E. *Alcohol and Youth: An Analysis of the Literature.* Report prepared for the National Institute on Alcohol Abuse and Alcoholism. NTIS PB-268-698/AS, March 1977.

Dawkins, M.P. Spatial patterns of alcohol outlets in the Washington, D.C., black community. *Proceedings of the Pennsylvania Academy of Science,* 53 (1): 89-97, 1979.

Dillin, J. Alcohol and television. *Christian Science Monitor,* June 30, 1975.

Jessor, R., and Jessor, S.L. Adolescent development and the onset of drinking. *Journal of Studies on Alcohol,* 36 (1): 27-51, 1975.

Karenga, R.M. *Essays on Struggle: Position and Analysis.* San Diego, Calif.: Kawaida Publication, 1978.

National Clearinghouse for Alcohol Information, National Institute on Alcohol Abuse and Alcoholism, by McManus and Kassebaum. *The Boys Harbor Alcohol Education Program.* Rockville, Md.: The Institute, 1977.

Nowlis, H. "Commonalities Among Prevention Programs for Children and Youth." Paper prepared for Alcohol, Drug Abuse, and Mental Health Administration Conference on Prevention, 1979.

Roizen, J. "Alcohol and Crime: The Relationship in Two Populations — Youths and Blacks." Paper prepared for a conference of the Law Enforcement Assistance Administration, Washington, D.C., Oct. 1979.

Strauss, Robert. *Alcohol and Society.* New York City, N.Y.: Insight Comunications, 1973.

Whitten, B. Untitled paper presented to Vocational Education Teachers Meeting, Baltimore, Md., 1976.

Chapter 9

PREVENTION AND TREATMENT OF BLACK ALCOHOLISM IN THE WORKPLACE

RAYMOND SANCHEZ MAYERS, PH.D.

CARANN SIMPSON FEAZELL, M.S.S.W.

INTRODUCTION

PROGRAMS attempting to deal with the problem of alcoholism in the workplace date back to the 1940s. While a few companies set up alcoholism treatment programs during this period, it was not until the 1950s that industry began to regard alcoholism as a significant problem (Surles, 1978:14). By the middle of the 1970s, the number of alcohol programs in industry had grown to over 600 (Saltman, 1977:13).

One factor in the growth of alcoholism treatment programs in industry was the growing awareness on the part of business people, as well as labor, of the tremendous loss of productivity due to alcohol-related problems. There are also enormous costs associated with alcohol abuse. For example, "the average alcohol problem person is said to cost $1,500 to $4,000 per year, to operate at 50 percent efficiency, and to average twenty-two days in lost time" (Lotterhos, 1975:7). Additional costs to industry include higher absenteeism,

The authors would like to thank Bernadine Foster, M.S.W., Area Director of the Massachusetts Department of Social Services, for her helpful comments.

poor decision-making, accidents, increased benefit costs, lost sales, safety hazards, lowered morale of other workers, to name just a few. Various studies have found that:

— Alcoholic employees have two and a half times as much absenteeism as their fellow employees.
— Alcoholic employees have accident rates 3.6 times that of other employees.
— Alcoholic employees collect over three times the amount of sickness payments as other employees.
— They have twice the incidence of respiratory and cardiovascular disease.
— They have three times the incidence of digestive and musculoskeletal disorders (Follman, 1976:82).

The passage of the Hughes Act in 1970 was another significant factor in the growth of treatment programs for alcohol abusing workers in industry. This Act authorized the establishment of the National Institute of Alcoholism and Alcohol Abuse (NIAAA). The Institute not only funded and encouraged research and treatment on all aspects of alcoholism, it was also attentive to the problems of alcoholic workers. In 1973 the Secretary of the Department of Health, Education and Welfare recommended that Congress pass legislation to undertake the early detection and treatment of problem drinkers in business and industry (Schramm, 1977:ix). It was also the involvement of the federal government that brought a shift in focus of the programs. In the early 1970s the NIAAA recommended the use of the "broad brush" approach in which assistance is provided to all employees with poor work performance whether the problem is alcohol related or not (Schramm, 1977:8). Today, alcoholism programs in industry have expanded to deal with the broad range of human problems that may manifest themselves in the workplace. These broader programs are called Employee Assistance Programs (EAP's), and over 57 percent of the Fortune 500 companies now have them (Segal et al., 1983:430). The NIAAA is continuing its interest in this area and has as one of its goals for 1990 that over 70 percent of major firms have EAP's. It has also begun to look at ways that employees in smaller firms can be covered by EAP's. Because of the diversity of industry, the EAP's currently in existence differ tremendously in terms of the number of employees involved, program structures, union involvement, availability of treatment and rehabilitation resources in the community, and level and quality of treatment personnel within the organization. However, there are commonalities with all programs. Thus, an Employee Assistance Program may be defined as:

> ". . . a system for identifying and treating a variety of medical or behavioral problems that might be responsible for an employee's poor job performance. Its main objective is to restore an employee to normal work behavior and productivity. By offering an alternative to being fired, EAP can help the employee to be a better producer for his employer as well as to function better as an individual" (Googins, 1975:465).

Although alcohol treatment programs in industry have moved to attempting to deal with a broader range of employee problems, the aims of employee assistance programs (EAP's) are consistent with those of the older alcohol programs as listed by the Conference Board in 1970 (Follman, 1976:120-121):

1. To lower costs
2. To reduce absenteeism
3. To improve production
4. To increase safety
5. To insure sounder decision-making
6. To retain the services of valuable employees
7. To build morale
8. To replace ineffective, punitive, disciplinary measures with problem-solving approaches.

Thus, an EAP program can be of benefit to all employees, black and white. If proper safeguards are instituted to protect the rights of workers, company policies can ensure that black employees are treated fairly and equitably in the process of trying to secure treatment for them. That is, in the past, black workers with drinking problems may have just been summarily fired. But now, the EAP may not only help them stop drinking, it may also make sure that they keep their job.

In this paper an overview of employee assistance programs, especially those features of EAP's that can be utilized to help the alcoholic employee will be discussed. Of particular concern are aspects of prevention and treatment in the workplace that may be applied to the black worker. To this end, a variety of strategies are presented within a framework of differing interpersonal lifestyles of blacks.

Components of Employee Assistance Programs

Follman (1976:129) has delineated the generally agreed upon components of a well-conceived alcoholism control program as including the following:

1. The full and active support of top management.
2. The formal establishment of a WRITTEN company policy on alcoholism.
3. The applicability of the program to employees at all levels, including executives.
4. Trained supervisory personnel and shop stewards functioning under written guidance.
5. Advice with respect to available treatment modalities.
6. Continuing communication with all employees.
7. Full and equal participating support by unions where these are involved.
8. Insurance protection against the costs of treatment and for time lost while undergoing treatment.
9. Confidentiality of all records.
10. A clear understanding that if work performance does not improve or if treatment is not accepted or followed, the job could be in jeopardy.
11. Continuing reevaluation of the program.

As was mentioned, there are a diversity of types of EAP's ranging from "in-house" programs to consortiums. But whatever the model used, the alcohol-abusing worker usually comes to the attention of the EAP because his or her supervisor has identified deteriorating work performance and has "confronted" the employee about it. The employee may also self-refer or be referred by family, coworkers, or the union. In discussing issues related to the black alcoholic worker, we will view these issues as the responsibility of the person in charge of the EAP, who should be trained in one of the helping professions. We have called this person the "EAP professional."

Treatment Approaches

Typically, in most EAP's treatment takes the form of diagnosis, assessment, crisis intervention, and information and referral. In terms of assessment and diagnosis, it must be remembered that the business organization's primary function is not a social welfare one. Therefore, its main concern is with worker productivity and factors that may interfere with the employee's functioning on the job. It is not concerned with cultural differences between blacks and other racial/ethnic groups; it is not concerned with cultural values regarding drinking. It is only concerned with disruptions to organizational productivity.

Crisis intervention may deal with any number of worker problems that crop up either on or off the job and that have a detrimental impact on the worker. This may include a host of problems that are many times alcohol-related, including spouse battering, child abuse, attempted suicide, accidents, and so forth. However, the primary concern of crisis intervention is not to impact the worker's culture, but to stabilize the immediate crisis and improve the employee's ability to cope.

The main function of the EAP professional, though, is to have knowledge of available community resources that can be used for information and referral. It is in this area of information and referral that we believe the EAP professional can be most helpful to the black alcoholic employee because effective use of referral sources is directly related to the organization's ability to provide adequate treatment for the worker's problem.

In a sense, the treatment of alcoholic workers in industry has been to some extent "color blind." That is, in companies with written and very formalized procedures, theoretically all employees are treated in the same manner. This may not have been the case in the past in many companies, especially those with less formalized procedures. Even with written procedures, informal influences may be brought to bear on decisions about the employee.

For instance, it is known that blacks are disproportionately underrepresented in traditional treatment programs both as counselors and as clients. They are not likely to seek out treatment unless confronted with a crisis situation such as the threat of loss of job

(Williams, 1982:32). And, as is the case in many community-based treatment programs, black clients seem to be underrepresented in referrals to EAP's. Some of the reasons cited for this underutilization of services are:

1. Inability to absorb costs when not included in insurance coverage;
2. Few black service providers on EAP staffs;
3. Programs oriented to white middle class;
4. Few blacks on policy-making committees for EAP's (Williams, 1982:35).

In order to be utilized by black employees, the Employee Assistance Program must demonstrate a sensitivity to the needs of the black employee. If neither the EAP itself or the programs it refers clients to have this sensitivity, then it is easy to understand why the black employee would not willingly utilize the EAP's services or actively participate in a rehabilitation program recommended by the EAP. For the alcoholic black worker, sensitivity to his or her needs involves knowledge of resources in the black community that can be utilized to provide support during the period of treatment as well as afterword.

Bell and Evans (1983) have developed a typology of interpersonal life-styles of blacks that can be useful for EAP counselors trying to develop resources for blacks with alcohol-related problems. We recognize that as human beings we are all highly complex. We know that not all blacks are homogeneous, that they vary in the beliefs, goals, ideals, religion, social class, and many of the other ways that Americans differ. This typology may be thought of as a continuum on which people may be found at different points. And, because of the highly dynamic nature of the human personality, a person may move from one category to another over time. Also, the categories within the typology tend to be highly related to education and social class. Given these caveats, let us turn to the typology:

1. Acculturated black

This person has taken on the values and ideals of the majority white culture and tends to reject black culture as inferior. He or she rejects customs, rituals, or concerns of blacks, and many react in a hostile manner when confronted with them. The acculturated black person tends to be upper middle class, lives in a predominantly white community, and works in a managerial or professional position with mostly whites.

2. Bicultural black

This person has pride in racial identity, black culture and traditions, yet is comfortable operating in the white world. He or she has learned to operate with some "cultural schizophrenia," and may return to the black community when highly stressed. Bicultural blacks' social needs can be met in either a black or white context; they tend to be middle class; live and work in integrated work settings.

3. Culturally-immersed black

This person tends to reject the dominant white culture and values. The behavior, mannerisms, and attitudes of this person are often termed "militant" by nonblacks. He or she also tends to use racial grounds for denial and rationalizing when confronted with stressful situations. Culturally-immersed blacks tend to differ widely in background, although many are from low-income inner city areas. The civil rights movement of the 1960s was a time when many middle-class black college students became culturally-immersed, and active in promoting the black cultural heritage. Many of these black activists are successful professionals today and more likely would be described as bicultural. The culturally-immersed individual may not be very successful by white standards. This client may be difficult for the white or even acculturated black counselor to work with because of extreme differences in views and the often angry feelings of the black toward white authority figures.

4. Traditional black

This person tends to have limited social contacts outside of the black community, even though he or she must depend on the white world for survival needs in terms of employment. The traditional black most often comes from a rural or poverty background and does not respond well to modern counseling techniques in which self-disclosure to strangers is required. Often the black church and extended family ties are important in his or her life (Bell and Evans, 1983:104-108).

Understanding this typology is an essential ingredient in developing black cultural sensitivity and may be useful in the matching of available resources to the needs of the black alcoholic worker. If the match between the black worker and the treatment option is contrary to the needs of the worker, or ignores these needs, then the success of the worker's rehabilitation has been jeopardized by the helper whose job it is to maximize the efforts and support for change. The need to successfully match worker's needs with resources is just as crucial in the aftercare/follow-up stage when the worker reenters the job situation and must face once more the stresses associated not only with the job, but with his or her family, racism and sexism, and living in a society that encourages the use of alcohol as a social lubricant.

The differences in cultural life-styles that exist among blacks are important dimensions in the coordination of treatment and prevention activities in working with black alcoholics. EAP professionals must be cognizant of the differences and pursue treatment strategies holistic in orientation. We suggest that the following perspectives on treatment and after care support are essential in effectively linking the alcoholic with available rehabilitation resources.

For the acculturated black worker, it would be best to look for a treatment center that projects a middle-class, Anglo atmosphere. Because of feelings about black inferiority, this client would not do well with a black counselor. Before issues regarding cultural identity are dealt with, the black alcoholic worker must be put on the road to recovery from alcoholism. Aftercare support, vital in all clients with chemical dependency, should be in a support group that is predominantly white. A principal support person should be a member of this worker's profession or peer group, possibly a recovering coworker. Family should be involved in the after care support, and within this family structure, the feelings about self-identity could be explored for their relationship to the drinking problem (See Table 9-1).

For the bicultural individual, a counselor or treatment modality that projects a middle-class image is more important than the racial make-up of the staff or other clients. A support person who has a common shared identity with the person, for example, a coworker, is

TABLE 9-1
Resources and Supports for Black Alcoholic Workers

Interpersonal Life Style	Appropriate Resource	Appropriate Support
Acculturated	Middle-class Anglo atmosphere	Recovering co-worker; or professional peer.
Bicultural	Middle-class either Anglo or black	Recovering co-worker Anglo or black; racially mixed AA group.
Culturally Immersed	Strong black community-based program	Recovering black activist;community leader;black self-help group.
Traditional	Religious sponsor	Recovering person in black/religious community.

more important than whether the person is black or white. A racially mixed AA group would also be helpful to the recovering bicultural black. Stresses of expectations in both the Anglo and black "worlds" will need to be addressed.

The culturally-immersed black alcoholic worker is the most difficult for the white counselor or treatment program to work with, indeed, this person would probably not even go to a white-oriented treatment center. Even black counselors will meet with resistance from this type of client. The counselor and/or treatment center must be able to address the injustice done to blacks without letting this become an excuse for the client's alcoholism. This type of black alcoholic needs to be in treatment on an in- or out-patient basis in a strong black community-based program. An appropriate aftercare support would be a recovering activist in the black community, or a tough, black-oriented self-help group.

The traditional black alcoholic worker would do best with a religiously-oriented treatment center or counselor sponsored by the black community. He or she tends to not do well with a person who cannot understand "black English" and feels uncomfortable in self-disclosure in a group (especially white) setting. The traditionalist needs follow-up to maintain recovery in an AA group of black, religious orientation. Additional supports for this person would be family members or a recovering alcoholic well respected in the black religious community.

We have included the above range of treatment options because some people assume that alcoholism is a leveler in which social class and race/ethnicity are irrelevant because of the common denominator — booze. But social class differences are relevant both in the implementation of an EAP (Trice and Beyer, 1977) and in the choice of treatment (Heyman, 1977). Also, the stereotype that most black alcoholics are "street people" and therefore "street people" should be included as counselors is nonsense (Beverly, 1976:97). As the Bell and Evans model tries to illustrate, there is a wide range of black interpersonal styles, and they must be matched with appropriate treatment and support for the best treatment and rehabilitation outcome. Finally, our discussion focused on working black alcoholics, and this includes everyone from the janitor of a company to a high-level executive. We submit that the black alcoholic executive would feel just as uncomfortable in treatment with the black "street-type person" as anyone else of similar social class background.

To find appropriate treatment programs for black alcoholic workers the EAP professional needs to liaison with social service agencies and community groups in black neighborhoods. Other possible sources of information are the local, county, and state councils on alcoholism. Task forces on black alcoholism have been set up in various communities and can be valuable resources as well. They may know which church groups are sponsoring support groups, and whether there are black AA groups in the community.

Prevention Approaches

Alcohol prevention programs in industry are geared toward heightening employee awareness to the health risks of excessive drinking, educational programs focusing on aspects of the disease, and continuing promotion of the EAP as the place to go with the problem. For prevention geared toward the black worker, some understanding of the dynamics of drinking within the black culture as well as an understanding of the culture of drinking within the work organization is involved (Fine et al., 1982).

The professional in charge of the EAP must also be aware of the stressors within the work environment and their impact on the black worker. To ignore these factors and focus only on the psychological and physiological aspects of the problem is only partializing it and to some extent, "blaming the victim."

Given the constraints of the corporate setting, there are still a number of preventive approaches that can be taken. These approaches may be termed "alcohol-specific and nonspecific strategies" (Williams, 1982:36). Alcohol-specific strategies in the workplace involve trying to influence drinking behavior through education. Educational programming in the workplace must be done by the EAP professional in conjunction with the training and medical departments. Some activities included here are seminars for employees, guest speakers at brown-bag lunches, development of media materials about alcohol abuse, dissemination of information about alcohol programs, and so forth.

Nonspecific strategies involve trying to influence drinking behavior by dealing with broader life-coping and problem-solving activities. Again, in conjunction with the medical and training departments, a wellness program for employees could be developed. The wellness program could include training on exercise, diet, handling stress, learning assertiveness, and provision of employee exercise rooms or jogging trails. And as we agree that "reaching today's black youth is the key to the solution of tomorrow's alcohol abuse and alcoholism problems in the black community" (Williams, 1982:36), there are other steps that corporations can take. In recognition that they have a social responsibility to their communities, many organizations are involved in corporate giving programs in which they donate money to nonprofit charitable organizations. Some of these donations could go to black community-based groups that are working on the prevention of alcohol and drug abuse in the black community, and especially to those groups working for the development of prevention programs aimed at young people.

Conclusion

Of extreme importance to program success is the personal insight of the EAP professional staff regarding their own values and prejudices as they affect their ability to deal effectively with the alcoholic employee. Bell and Evans mention counseling styles that range from overtly racist and hostile to color blind to culturally-liberated. The distinction between being color blind and culturally-sensitive is an important one for the EAP counselor. The color blind counselor is committed to equality of all peoples, no matter what their color or ethnic background. But in choosing to disregard the color of the client's skin, the counselor is negating the black cultural experience as a meaningful part of the client's life history and therefore negating the self-identity of the client (Wright et al., 1983).

The culturally-sensitive counselor does not disregard racial or cultural differences, rather is aware of them and their impact on the client and the helping relationship. The culturally-aware counselor appreciates the differences and similarities among and between cultures and uses this knowledge positively in the counseling intervention.

It is the responsibility of the EAP professional to ensure that workers with deteriorating performance are handled fairly and equitably, without prejudice. One way to identify possible discrimination is to evaluate sources of referral, looking for "hot spots" where referrals are primarily and consistently of minority workers. But the EAP person must also make sure that proper procedures involving documentation of decreased work performance has been carried out. Recognition of the stressors that may impact on minority workers and focusing on alternative ways to deal with these stressors is also the job of the EAP professional.

Finally, the EAP professional should strive to ensure that not only the EAP, but the entire company, is sensitive to the needs of all employees, black and white. And in utilizing culturally relevant resources, the chances of successful recovery and return to productivity are increased for the black alcohol-abusing worker.

REFERENCES

Alcoholism and employee relations: a BNA special report. Washington,

D.C., Bureau of National Affairs, 1978.

Bell, Peter and Evans, Jimmy: Counseling the black client, pp. 100-121 in
T.D. Watts and R. Wright Jr. *Black Alcoholism*. Springfield, Charles C
Thomas, 1983.

Beverly, Creigs C.: Toward a model for training black alcoholic counselors,
pp. 87-98 in F.D. Harper (ed.). *Alcohol Abuse and Black America*. Alexandria, Douglass, 1976.

Coney, John Charles: The precipitating factors in the use of alcoholic treatment services: a comparative study of black and white alcoholics. San
Francisco, R & E Research Associates, 1977.

Fine, Michelle, Akabas, Sheila H., and Bellinger, Susan: Cultures of
drinking: a workplace perspective. *Social Work*, 27(5):436-440, 1982.

Follman, Joseph F.: Alcoholics and business. New York, AMACOM,
1976.

Googins, Bradley: Employee assistance programs. *Social Work*, 20: 464-467,
1975.

Googins, Bradley and Kurtz, Norman R.: Factors inhibiting supervisory
referrals to occupational alcoholism intervention programs. *Journal of
Studies on Alcohol*, 41(11):1196-1208, 1980.

Harper, Frederick D. (Ed.): *Alcohol Abuse and Black America*. Alexandria,
Douglass Publishers, 1976.

Heyman, Margaret M.: *Alcoholism Programs in Industry*. New Brunswick,
Rutgers Center of Alcohol Studies, 1978.

Lotterhos, Jerry F.: Historical and sociological perspectives of alcohol-
related problems, pp. 3-39 in R.L. Williams and G.H. Moffat. *Occupational Alcoholism Programs*. Springfield, Charles C Thomas, 1975.

Saltman, Jules: *Drinking on the Job*. New York, Public Affairs Committee,
1977.

Schramm, Carl J.: *Alcoholism and Its Treatment in Industry*. Baltimore, Johns
Hopkins University Press, 1977.

Segal, Mel, Palsgrove, Gary, Sevy, Thomas D., and Collins, Thomas E.:
The 1990 prevention objectives for alcohol and drug misuse: progress
report. Public Health Reports, 98(5):426-435, 1983.

Smith, Cedric M.: *Alcoholism: Treatment*, Volume 2, 1977. Montreal, Annual Research Reviews, Eden Press, 1978.

Surles, Carol Diann Smith: *Historical Development of Alcoholism Control Programs in Industry from 1940-1978*. Ann Arbor, University Microfilms,
1981.

Trice, Harrison M.: Applied research studies: job-based alcoholism and
employee assistance programs. *Alcohol Health and Research World*, 4(3):4-
16, 1980.

Trice, Harrison M. and Beyer, Janice M.: Differential use of an alcoholism policy in federal organizations by skill level of employees, pp. 44-68 in C. J. Schramm (ed.). *Alcoholism and Its Treatment in Industry*. Baltimore, Johns Hopkins University Press, 1977.

Watts, Thomas D. and Wright, Roosevelt Jr. (Eds.): *Black Alcoholism: Toward a Comprehensive Understanding*. Springfield, Charles C Thomas, 1983.

Williams, Millree: Blacks and alcoholism: issues in the 1980s. *Alcohol Health and Research World*, 6(4):31-40, 1982.

Williams, Richard L. and Moffat, Gene H.: *Occupational Alcoholism Programs*. Springfield, Charles C Thomas, 1975.

Wright, Roosevelt, Jr.; Saleebey, Dennis; Watts, Thomas D. and Lecca, Pedro J.: *Transcultural Perspectives in the Human Services*. Springfield, Charles C Thomas, 1983.

Chapter 10

THE UTILIZATION OF MINISTERS AS ALCOHOL COUNSELORS AND EDUCATORS: INCREASING PREVENTION AND TREATMENT RESOURCES IN THE BLACK COMMUNITY

CAROLYN F. SWIFT PH.D.

SETHARD BEVERLY, M.DIV.

INTRODUCTION

ALCOHOL abuse is the number one health problem in the black community (Harper, 1976; King, 1983). The problem is particularly acute for young black adults: the mortality rate for 25 to 34-year-olds is over ten times the rate for white youth (Maline, Munch and Archer, 1978). In addition, research shows that black youth are rapidly increasing heavy drinking. Alcohol is involved in most violent crimes and in 50 percent of deaths from traffic accidents in the black community (Harper, 1976). The mental health consequences of alcoholism fall disproportionately on blacks. These

This project was partically supported through 314 d funds provided by the Department of Health, Education and Welfare. The authors wish to thank Elizabeth Gray, Walt Meyer and Andrew Rollins, Jr. for their continued support and encouragement throughout the project.

conditions include cancer, malnutrition, pulmonary disease, hypertension, and birth defects (Williams, 1982). Christmas (1978) relates the increasing incidence of chronic alcoholism in minority communities to "the lack of services that are culturally consonant or effectively linked to potential support systems within the minority community," and . . . "late entry into the health system, limited access because of poverty, racial barriers, or the lack of specific services and minority group resistance to viewing alcohol abuse as a problem" (1978, p. 21).

Attempts to treat black patients through outreach programs designed for and primarily used by the white community have been singularly unsuccessful. While alcoholism helpers should have knowledge of the social, economic, and cultural realities of the lives of minority alcoholics, few programs have been staffed with helpers equipped to serve minority populations. The results of this lack of resources is that most black alcoholics receive no treatment at all. This chapter describes a program in which black ministers were invited to assist in attempting to provide resources to confront the problem of black alcoholism in a midwestern community.

Religious leaders — rabbis, ministers, and priests — serve as spiritual teachers, counselors, and general resources on matters of this world and the next for their religious communities. Their roles vary widely from community to community. Religious faith, economic class, and geographic location account for some of the variations. Ethnicity is a major determinant of the ways in which religious leaders relate to the communities they serve. The history of slavery and Christianity superimposed on tribal religions and customs, compounded by the devastating effects of discrimination, have shaped the unique role of the minister and the church in the black community in the United States (Simpson, 1978).

Black ministers and black churches have traditionally served as core resources for their community's human services. This tends to be the case for both direct and indirect delivery of such services. The black church has traditionally served as a community center. Simpson (1978) notes that the church has functioned as a clearinghouse, a meeting place and a mutual aid center.

Black ministers are noted for their action orientation. Wilmore

(1972) traces this to the founding of the independent Negro church in the late eighteenth century. The efforts of black ministers to feed the poor, for example, tend toward the community-wide collection and distribution activities exemplified on a large scale by Jesse Jackson's Chicago programs. The black minister's action orientation is seen in the personal services performed for parishioners, as in taking an unemployed parishioner to a job interview, or interceding with the social service system for a member caught in the bureaucracy.

This call to action often extends beyond individual parishioners and beyond parish boundaries to the broader arena of community problems. Simpson cites a group of ministers whose work in the sixties focused on community concerns . . . "Milton Galamison, who was active in the instigation of the New York City school boycotts; Gardner Taylor, who served as a member of the New York City Board of Education; Obadiah Dempsey, a leader in the fight against narcotic addiction and drug traffic in New York City; Eugene Callender, who was active in Harlem Neighborhoods Association; and Leon Sullivan, leader of boycotts against businesses that had employed few or no Negroes and organizer of the Opportunities Industrialization Centers to train and place unemployed blacks in Philadelphia and other cities" (1978, p. 242).

Martin Luther King and Jesse Jackson have carried their ministries beyond national boundaries to plead the cause of people of color, and those disenfranchised by discrimination, around the globe. Black ministers, then, constitute a major resource for both their minority communities and the larger social surrounding. Their potential for linking the religious communities they serve with social services and other community resources has been largely ignored by the majority community. The study described below, previously unpublished, was conducted in the early seventies in a midwestern city with a 20 percent black population. Alcoholism had been defined by city officials as a major community problem. They were particularly concerned that something be done about the revolving door misdemeanor alcoholic offender, and requested assistance from the local mental health center and the jail chaplain in addressing the problem. A series of community interventions resulted. This report describes only those which enlisted the aid of black ministers to increase the prevention and treatment resources for alcohol problems in the black community.

A community survey of persons over 65 showed a dramatic difference between the white and black populations with regard to perceived treatment resources for alcohol-related problems. An overwhelming majority (80 percent) of white senior citizens reported Alcoholics Anonymous to be a major resource, while none cited local churches as a place to turn to for help with alcohol-related problems. Survey results showed just the opposite in the black community. Almost 80 percent of the black respondents reported their church as a major resource and none named Alcoholics Anonymous.

In an attempt to strengthen existing resource networks in the black community and to provide a preventive approach to alcohol-related problems, a clergy workshop was conducted to educate the clergy concerning alcoholism, its economic and sociological correlates, and counseling techniques with alcohol-troubled persons. The program codirectors had established roles as consultants within the local court-jail and mental systems: a white female psychologist and a black minister who also served as jail chaplain. As an outgrowth of the workshop, two separate but related programs were established: the Court Counselor Aide program, in which black ministers provided counseling for misdemeanor offenders, and a court class in alcoholism, which utilized the ministers in teacher/therapist roles.

COURT COUNSELOR AIDES

Program Description

The codirectors arranged for six black ministers who had participated in the workshop to be appointed as "court counselor aides" by the judge of the municipal court. They were selected because of their expressed interest in volunteering to work with the court to develop treatment alternatives to incarceration for black offenders with alcohol-related problems. Each of the ministers agreed to conduct five counseling sessions each month with this population. This provided the city's first one-to-one counseling service for indigent black alcoholics. Monthly team meetings provided a forum to discuss counseling techniques as well as specific cases. It was anticipated that at the end of the year the experience and training the ministers received in counseling alcoholics, and in working with the court system, would qualify them as experts to function within the community as an articulate force working toward improved treatment programs. While the project did not have the monetary resources to reimburse the ministers the full value of their services, a grant was received to provide them with honoraria of $10 per counsel session and $10 per monthly team meeting. Referrals to the ministers were through the program directors. Typically, one of the directors met with the offender after sentencing, explained the counseling program, facilitated the official parole and called the minister to confirm the scheduled appointed time.

Working the politically sensitive setting of the local city hall created problems in implementation that could not fully have been anticipated. For example, the program suffered delays and internal problems as a result of a change in political administration. A city election removed the incumbent mayor and the new mayor replaced the police chief and the judges as well as other officers of the court. The directors then had to educate the new personnel with regard to the program. Several judges served before one was selected as permanent municipal court judge. The alcohol counseling program was in a state of flux during this time, since the approval of the judge was necessary to parole offenders. As a result, for a period of three to four months, few offenders were referred to the program.

Once the new officials were settled in, they made policy changes which created additional complications. The new judge ordered an increase in the rate at which days in jail were applied to reduce fines: from $1 per day to $10 per day. Prior to this, offenders were routinely fined $25 for public drunkenness. If indigent, the offender was obliged to spend 25 days in jail. At the new rate, offenders could work off the customary $25 fine in 2½ days. If offenders were picked up Friday night — and weekends were and continue to be peak periods for alcoholic offenses — and arraigned or tried in court, they were out by Monday noon under the new system. By the time prisoners were interviewed and offered a parole to one of the ministers, they had essentially paid the fine by spending one or two days in jail and were not inclined to obligate future time voluntarily. Thus, the reforms instituted by the judge overturned the balance between sentence and parole by removing the levers on which the Court Counselor Aide Program was based. These complications in program implementation are described here to provide the appropriate context for interpretation of results, and to alert hardy souls who would intervene in local governmental settings to the sorts of unanticipated events that overturn the best-laid experimental plans.

Despite these complications, the program achieved its major objectives. Fifty-two persons were counseled directly by the ministers, with family members and friends involved as additional lateral components of their caseloads. Most offenders were seen more than once, so these figures do not reflect actual number of counseling sessions. Seventy-two percent of the parolees counseled were male. A fourth of those counseled were under 25 years of age, 38 percent were 26 to 40, another 38 percent were 41 to 60, and none was over 60.

For most of the black offenders who participated, the ministers provided the first attempts at formal counseling directed to their alcohol problems. Referral to other resources was restrictive, since, as noted above, the organization of Alcoholics Anonymous was not viewed as a resource by the black community. At that point in its history, the local AA group had neither actively sought nor welcomed black members.

The ministers, themselves, often continued their relationships with the offenders assigned to them beyond the number of sessions set in the program. The helping role adopted by the ministers was broadened from counseling to direct intervention with agencies — such as Social Security, welfare, employment agencies and hospitals — on behalf of their clients. These activities resulted in increased benefits, jobs, and admissions to treatment for their clinets. The personal relationship which developed between minister and client permitted innovations and risk-taking on the part of the minister, with consequent benefits in treatment outcome. Many of the ministers encouraged their clients to call them in a crisis, no matter what the hour. This invitation was accepted and tested. Several ministers routinely made personal calls on their clients. Others supplied transportation at crucial times — such as job interviews or to visit a sick relative or friend. One account is vividly recalled in which a minister, visiting the home of an aging exboxer alcoholic, poured a gallon of whiskey down the sink before the old man's eyes. The minister attributes his action to inspiration. The directors attribute his safety to divine intervention, since the alcoholic had a history of repeated arrests for assault. Incidents such as these were shared at the monthly team meetings.

At these monthly meetings, difficult cases were presented, advice was sought and given and factual information concerning the effects of alcohol on the body and the disease concept of alcoholism was provided. The information supplied to the court counselor aides, both in team meetings and in pamphlets and books, was designed for use in educating alcoholic offenders to the causes and consequences of alcohol abuse.

One of the projected goals of the program was to provide the ministers with education and experience in alcohol counseling with the hope that they would function outside the scope of the program to educate the public and use their skills in other community settings, thus supplying the community with indigenous resources in dealing with the problem of alcohol abuse. During the course of the program, three of the ministers were asked to speak to other groups or agencies concerning this work. It was also hoped that the ministers would increase their contact with the municipal court as a result of the program. Five of the six ministers visited the court and assumed helping roles in cases unrelated to the program. Three visited the jail and volunteered to serve as parole supervisors for offenders. This increased participation occurred during the course of the program when morale was high and the feedback of the team meetings supported experimentation and commitment. Since the program has ended, these activities have also dropped off, leading to the conclusion that some minimum skeleton system of feedback, reinforcement, and role legitimation must be maintained to keep persons drawn temporarily into the orbit of the court-jail system working within the system.

While continuing identification with the court-jail system has decreased since the termination of the program, the ministers have continued to be active in providing leadership to bring alcohol services to the community. Several of the ministers who participated in this program subsequently served on citizens' advisory committees of alcohol programs in the community, and as counselors and consultants in a 24-hour information and referral service and halfway house for alcoholics in the black community.

Other positive results of the program were the interest, goodwill, and respect generated between the program and the community, and the officials of the court and the ministers involved. There is no way to measure this accurately. However, various developments and events support the conclusion. For example, ministers not included in the original group learned of the program and called to ask the directors how they could become part of it. On several occasions the directors were approached by city officals who requested that the ministers be consulted about some issue related to the alcohol counseling program. These occasions illustrate the prominence of the group as a liaison between city officials and the black community during the vacuum of communications which followed the change-over in political administration. Wives and parents of alcoholics in the community called to ask how their husbands or sons could qualify for counseling with the court counselor aides; they had learned of the program through a relative or neighbor.

Results

Evaluation of the program involved follow-up questionnaires to those paroled to the program to check job changes, marital changes, drinking patterns, etc. and a comparison of conviction records of parolees for the year prior to and the year following counseling. Attempts to locate participants following their termination proved to be extremely difficult. Few had telephones, so that direct mail contact was the primary method used. Personal interviews were conducted with a few, but here, again, the lack of a telephone and inadequate addresses thwarted attempts at finding offenders in order to conduct interviews. A questionnaire was mailed to all participants. While direct mail surveys with alcoholic offenders carry a notoriously low rate of return, this method seemed the most viable means of making a contact. Below is a percentage breakdown of the returns of the questionnaire:

Questionnaires returned 11%
Undelivered questionnaires 39%
      moved, no forwarding address 17%
      unknown 16%
      nonexistent address 6%
No response to questionnaires 50%

It is obvious that no significant conclusions can be drawn from the small sample returning the questionnaire. Aside from the deficient number of those reporting, their representativeness must be questioned: returned questionnaires uniformly reported reduced drinking, stable employment and improvements in economic and/or social conditions. It is assumed that those less fortunate — i.e., those whose drinking problem resulted in job losses, divorce, etc. — were not motivated to return the questionnaire.

A large proportion of alcoholic offenders have no permanent address. They move from community to community, rarely putting down roots. The difficulties in locating such offenders one year after contact make collection of accurate follow-up data problematic. Fifty percent of the sample, however, must be assumed to have received the questionnaire but failed to return it, since these were not returned by the post office. In these cases the address is assumed to be accurate. With adequate manpower it would be feasible to recontact these offenders to collect the follow-up data. However, the number of return calls to a particular address to find the party at home and the necessity of selecting times outside of business hours to coincide with the offenders' at-home hours would require manpower beyond the scope provided by this project.

Records in the city's police department were not computerized at the time of this study, so comparison of conviction records had to be done by hand, tallying cases through visual inspection of the offenders' cards. In some cases cards were missing or false names were given when the offender entered the program, thus making it impossible to check that person's records. Special problems were involved in analyzing the data to determine the impact of counseling sessions with the ministers. This resulted from the fact that many persons were referred for parole whose misdemeanor offense was not labeled on the official record as alcohol-related, although alcohol was a contributing factor. Therefore, these data were analyzed two ways: first, alcoholic offenses for the year prior to and the year following termination of counseling; second, all offenses for the year prior to and the year following termination of counseling. According to both analyses there were significantly fewer convictions for offenses the year following termination of counseling. The evidence supports the conclusion that counseling and personal services provided by the black ministers were effective in reducing recidivism in this group of black offenders with alcohol-related problems.

COURT CLASS IN ALCOHOLISM

Program Description

One evening each week for a year, a class on alcoholism was conducted in the city's municipal courtroom. Participants were drawn from several populations:

1. Persons convicted of offenses involving alcohol and paroled to attend the class instead of serving jail sentences or paying fines.
2. Persons convicted of offenses involving alcohol and currently serving sentences but permitted to attend the class under proper guard.
3. Family members of parolees or prisoners.
4. Occasional police officers.
5. The general public.

While filling the role of an educational treatment program for persons in the community with alcohol-related problems, the class functioned primarily as a treatment alternative to incarceration for alcoholic offenders. The grant directors served as lecturer-therapists for the group. A succession of rotating guest therapists was drawn primarily from the ranks of the ministers who attend the clergy workshop, although representatives from Alcoholics Anonymous, the National Council on Alcoholism and Seven Steps were also used. While the parolees and prisoners were the most obvious target popu-

lation, the guest therapists comprised a second target population recruited to counsel in this field. The role of guest therapist, with an
honorarium of $30 per session, provided official sanction of the city
administration to welcome the guest therapist as an official member
of the treatment team. This formal recognition of the person's expertise was designed to reinforce their functioning in a helping role and,
hopefully, to lead the guest therapist to increased responsiveness to
the community's alcohol problems. It was hoped also that a positive
experience in this role would lead guest therapists to become more
directly involved in municipal court parole programs as well.

Each class began with a short lecture concerned with some phase
— physiological, psychological, social, or economic — of alcoholism, followed by a group therapy session focusing on but not limited
to the content of the lecture. Group therapy, role-playing, and films
were used as therapeutic and didactic techniques.

The same delays and internal problems experienced by the Court
Counselor Aide Program as a result of the change in political administration caused problems for the court class. Judges unfamiliar
with the options failed to make use of this parole program. Several
unanticipated events occurred that reduced the effectiveness of the
class. First, two "nonalcoholic" prisoners escaped from the class —
neither of whom should have been allowed to attend. Prior to the establishment of the class, procedures were set up with jail personnel
through proper administrative channels to insure that only offenders
with alcohol-related crimes be allowed to attend from the jail. Since
the municipal court tries only misdemeanor offenses, it was also ordered that no felons be allowed to attend. Jail personnel, particularly
booking desk officers, were designated to screen prospective class
members to eliminate violent or sick prisoners, or others constitut-
ing security risks.

However, one night a new and inexperienced jailer was left in
charge of the booking desk. He called out a blanket invitation to all
interested parties behind bars to attend the alcohol class. Not surprising, a majority of the prisoners responded, including several felons whose violent crimes were totally unrelated to alcohol. Because
of the unusually large size of the group, the session ended before the
director discovered their presence. At the end of the class, two felons
mixed with a crowd arriving to attend another meeting and in the

ensuing confusion escaped from the custody of the officer charged with returning the offenders to their cells. The incongruity of the two teetotaling prisoners attending the alcohol class and escaping in a crowd of 3-2 Little League Baseball Club members made for much merriment in local press rooms and behind the scenes, as well as red faces in the police department. An investigation of the incident fastened the blame on the errant booking desk officer. However, understandably, the police administration was unhappy. No prisoners were allowed to attend the class for four or five weeks following the incidents.

From the point of view of police administration, it is far simpler to lock up violators and release them only after sentences have been served. The complications involved in introducing treatment programs during incarceration require extra time and effort in working out procedures and training personnel. Greater security risks lead to greater opportunities for bungling with the resultant public embarrassment when something goes wrong. While the program directors tried to troubleshoot routine procedures initially, these procedures were not fail-safe, as demonstrated in the above incident.

Programs such as this, operating in the public eye of a large city jail and court system, depend for their success on the cooperation of officials involved. If the program is not supported actively, it must at least be tolerated by the system. Opposition on any level results in obstructions ranging from major blocks to the more subtle but equally effective annoyance of inaction. In this case, no sabotage was involved. The program had support at every level. The incident was the end result of a series of accidents.

The court class had an attendance of 613, summing the number of parolees and prisoners at each session across twelve months. Family, AA members and visitors from the public at large raised the total attendance figure to 822. Ninety-five percent of the parolees and prisoners attending were male. Participants were slightly older than those paroled to the Court Counselor Aide Program. Only 9 percent were under 25 years of age, 40 percent were 26 to 40, 46 percent were 41 to 60 and 5 percent were over 60 years of age. The class served as an introduction to treatment for many participants. Many continued to return to the class past the required number of sessions. After completion of their parole to the class, many transferred to AA groups or to therapy at the mental health center. As a result of discussions between the AA guest therapists, the black ministers and program directors involved in the Court Class Program, a rapprochement was initiated that resulted eventually in the increased availability of AA as a treatment resource for black alcoholics in the community. To a certain devoted number of faithful 10-15 persons over the year the class became a social club. It was actually referred to this way by several of the members who established rules of behavior for the club, censuring newcomers who took the club lightly or who did not show proper respect for fellow members. At the time the class was terminated these faithful members were concerned about their ability to remain sober without the support of the class. Many suggested that such "clubs" be established in various neighborhoods throughout the urban area. Three persons offered locations — places where such groups could meet. The information disseminated in the class served to educate participants to the effects of alcohol on the body as well as on behavior. Many subscribed to false myths concerning the use of alcohol. Films, pamphlets and brief lectures were the instruction techniques used.

The class provided an accepting, nonjudgmental audience for persons unaccustomed to attention. Participants shared current problems, past histories and advice on how to handle problems focusing on alcohol addiction. The processes of group therapy operated to provide a release for the expressed feelings of the participants. However, the constant influx of new members and termination of those completing paroles made for problems in group coherence from session to session.

The therapeutic effects that occur when one patient "helps" another are well known (Riessman, 1969). Although not postulated as a goal when the class was planned, it turned out that one of the most positive results was the undertaking of helpful behavior toward each other on the part of group members. They arranged to pick each other up for the class or give rides home, to run errands for those in jail, to cash checks, give cigarettes, make bonds, fill prescriptions, call relatives or visit spouses, etc. Once a member had performed such a service for another he seemed to be "hooked" into the class. Such personal commitment of time and effort served to give meaning to the otherwise directionless lives of men who had long since lost contact with any sort of meaningful "other." The class became a focal point in the lives of certain marginally skid row alcoholics, providing a reason for staying sober and an occasion for meeting others whose lives paralleled theirs.

The expectation that the guest therapists would become more directly involved in municipal court parole programs was realized. Nine of the therapists subsequently attended court sessions and offered their services to judges in working with offenders. Many asked how they could increase their expertise in the field of alcoholism, and expressed appreciation for the pamphlets, books, and films that were a part of the program. One participating black minister now serves as a part-time volunteer counselor in a rehabilitation program for young offenders operated by the court. Another has since taken part in a police-minority-group seminar. Involving minority leaders to work within the system was, in this instance, a seeding process resulting in the extension of their influence to other parts of the system. The ministers who participated said that the experience also helped them in developing sermons on this topic — an activity with clear prevention potential — as well as in counseling parishoners with alcohol problems.

Results

As with the court counselor aides, attempts to locate offenders proved to be difficult. Here, again, direct mail contact was the primary method used. A questionnaire was mailed to all participants. Below is a percentage breakdown of the returns of the questionnaire:

Questionnaires returned 6%
Undelivered questionnaires 32%
    deceased 2%
    moved, no forwarding address 20%
    unknown 4%
    nonexistent address 6%
No response to questionnaires 62%

Below is a comparison of conviction records for the year prior to and the year following participation in the class. Accurate data were available for 118 offenders. These persons had a total of 774 convictions for either public drunkenness or drunken driving up to the time they entered the court class.

> Number of convictions for public drunkenness or drunken driving for the 12-month period prior to entrance in the court class (N = 118) 233
>
> Number of convictions for public drunkenness or drunken driving for the 12-month period following termination from the court class (N = 118) 42

In analyzing the data it is necessary to take account of the fact that during the year following the Court Class Program law enforcement personnel were prohibited from arresting persons for public drunkenness due to a change in the state law. In our sample of 118, 97 persons had been out of the program a full year as of this legislative change. Comparisons of their convictions for alcoholic offenses for the year prior to and the year following participation in the court class were made. This was done by means of normal curve functions through the computation of a z score based on the differences between each offender's before and after record. The number of convictions following the court class was significantly less than the number of convictions in the year preceding the class (p. .01). While no arrests for public drunkenness were made after the new law went into effect, the police department maintained a card file listing name, address, date, age and place taken for persons picked up for drunkenness and transported to treatment centers or holding stations subsequent to the change. Of the 21 persons from the sample of 118 who had not been out of the program one year when the new law took effect, 7 persons (accounting for 10 separate incidents) were listed in this file at the end of the program year. The 10 incidents were treated as convictions and combined with the posttreatment data of the 97 described above in order to analyze the full sample of 118 on whom accurate data were available. Scores were computed for the differences in number of convictions for alcoholic offenses for the 12 months preceding and following treatment. Again, number of convictions following the court class was significantly less than the number of convictions in the year preceding the class (p .01). The evidence supports the hypothesis that forcing alcoholic offenders to attend a series of educational-therapeutic sessions reduces recidivism in this group. These results are also consistent with those from the Court Counselor Aide Program, demonstrating the efficacy of utilizing black ministers as alcohol counselors and educators.

SUMMARY

The two projects described in this report constitute a pilot project designed to test the practicality and effectiveness of utilizing black ministers to counsel offenders with alcohol-related problems in the setting of a Municipal Court and jail.

The court counselor aides and the court class were effective in:

- increasing treatment options for black alcoholics in the community;
- producing a corps of black ministers whose involvement as leaders in municipal Court alcohol programs spread to other areas of the community;
- reducing recidivism in offenders with alcohol-related problems. This represents an economic savings to the city in police time, court time, jail expenses, record keeping, etc. There is also the savings in fewer jobs lost and disrupted social relationships assumed to accompany reduced recidivism;
- providing education and therapy to offenders with alcohol-related problems;
- providing an alternative to incarceration.

REFERENCES

Christmas, J.J. Alcoholism services for minorities: Training issues and concerns. *Alcohol Health and Research World, 2*(3), Spring, 1978, 20-27.

Harper, F. D., ed. *Alcohol Abuse in Black America.* Alexandria, VA: Douglass Publishers, 1976.

King, L. M. Alcoholism: Studies Regarding Black Americans 1977-1980. *Alcohol and Health Monograph 4, Special Population Issue*, Washington, D.C.: PHS publication.

Maline, H. J.; Munch, N. E.; and Archer, L. D. A national surveillance system for alcoholism and alcohol abuse. Paper presented at the 32nd International Congress on Alcoholism and Drug Dependence, Warsaw, Poland, September, 1978. As found in "Alcohol and Blacks," *Alcohol Topics in Brief*, RP0300. Rockville, MD: National Clearinghouse for Alcohol Information.

Riessman, F., The helper therapy principle. In Bernard G. Guerney, Ed., *Psychotherapeutic Agents: New Roles for Nonprofessionals, Parents and Teachers*. Holt, Rinehart and Winston, 1969, 87-95.

Simpson, G. E. *Black Religions in the New World*. New York: Columbia University Press, 1978.

Williams, M. Blacks and alcoholism: Issues in the 1980s. *Alcohol Health and Research World*, 6(4): Summer, 1982, 31-40.

Wilmore, Gayraud. *Black Religion and Black Radicalism*. Garden City, NY: Doubleday, 1972.

NAME INDEX

A

Aarens, M., 38, 45
Abelson, H. I., 123, 138
Akabas, Sheila H., 178, 180
Alken, H., 91, 104
Amundsen, A., 36, 46
Aponte, J. F., 10
Archer, L. D., 182, 197
Atkinson, C., 100, 106
Austin, G. A., 84, 87

B

Bachman, J. G., 124, 138
Bacon, S. D., 32, 49, 55, 63
Bader, B. C., 9
Bailey, M. P., 91, 104
Barsby, S. L., 36, 46
Baumohl, Jim, 68, 69, 70, 79
Beauchamp, D. E., ix, xv, 10, 34, 35, 46
Begleiter, H., xv, 46, 68, 63
Bell, D. S., 63
Bell, Peter, 105, 155, 160, 167, 173, 175, 177, 179, 180
Bell, R. A., 10
Bellinger, Susan, 178, 180
Belous, R. S., 113, 121
Benjamin, M., xiii, xv
Benjamin, R., xiii, xv
Benedict, Ruth, 153
Benrud, C. D., 123, 125, 139
Bentley, J. T., 119, 120
Beverly, Creigs, C., 65, 80, 177, 180
Beverly, Sethard, 86, 182

Beyer, Janice M., 177, 181
Biron, R. M., 43, 50
Blacker, E., 56, 63
Bland, John, 24, 25
Blane, H. T., xii, xiii, xv, 34, 37, 40, 46, 59, 63, 84, 87, 123, 124, 138, 143, 167
Blocker, T. S., 47
Bloom, Martin, 5, 9
Bourne, P. G., 89, 105, 108, 119, 120, 122, 138
Brehm, M. L., 123, 125, 139
Brisbane, Frances L., 6, 9
Brunn, K., 54, 63
Bryce, F. O., 124, 138

C

Cahalan, Don, 32, 37, 46, 94, 96, 105, 109, 120, 150
Caldwell, Fulton J., 20, 21, 30, 62, 63
Calender, Eugene, 184
Callicut, James W., 9
Cameron, T., 38, 40, 45, 46
Carpenter, J. A., xvi, 87
Carroll, E. E., 84, 87
Carter, Ruther, 29
Catalano, R., 110, 120
Cavanaugh, B., 123, 125, 139
Cavanaugh, E. R., 123, 125, 139
Chafetz, Morris, 57
Chase, J. A., 125, 138
Chatham, Lois, 23, 24
Christmas, J. J., 62, 64, 183, 197
Cisin, I. H., 32, 46, 94, 96, 105, 109, 120, 123, 138

J

Jackson, Jesse, 184
Jessor, R., xiii, xvi, 37, 47, 52, 53, 58, 59, 62, 64, 85, 87, 100, 125, 128, 138, 139, 143, 167
Jessor, S. L., xiii, xvi, 37, 47, 52, 53, 58, 59, 62, 64, 100, 125, 128, 132, 138, 143, 167
Johnson, B. D., 84, 87
Johnson, J. H., 105
Johnson, Reverend, 153
Johnston, L. D., 124, 138
Jones, R. L., 106

K

Kaelber, C. T., 124, 125, 128, 138
Kail, Barbara Lynn, 85, 108
Kalant, H., 47, 105
Kane, G. P., xvi
Karenga, Ron M., 151, 167
Kassebaum, 167
Keil, T. J., 95, 105
Kenward, K., xii, xvii
Ketter, R. F., 9
Kibuka, E. P., 70, 79
Kiloh, L. G., 63
Kinder, B. N., 40, 47
King, Louis M., ix, xvi, 14, 30, 74, 80, 99, 105, 121, 182, 197
King, Martin Luther, 184
King, Shirley Wesley, 7, 9, 85, 89, 109, 118, 121
Kissin, B., xv, 46, 48, 63
Klatsky, A. L., 96, 105
Klein, Donald C., 9
Klerman, G., 33, 34, 44, 47
Knupfer, G., 94, 105
Kornaczewski, A., 36, 49
Kramer, M., 95, 106
Kuller, L., 91, 106
Kurtz, Norman R., 170, 180
Kuusi, P., 36, 47

L

Lambert, S., 49
Larkins, J., ix, xvi
Lebeaux, C. N., 66, 79

Lecca, Pedro J., 6, 9, 11, 179, 180, 181
Ledermann, 54
Leffall, L. D., 91, 106
Lettieri, D. J., 84, 87
Levitan, S. A., 113, 121
Light, L., xvi, 47, 48, 49, 64, 108, 119, 120, 122, 138
Lilienfield, A., 91, 106
Lin, E., 10
Lipscomb, W. R., 108, 119, 121
Littles, Robbie, 26, 27
Locke, B. L., 95, 106
Lotterhos, Jerry F., 168, 180
Lowenfish, S. K., 95, 106
Lowman, C., 124, 125, 128, 138
Lumio, M., 34, 35, 36, 46

M

Mackay, J. R., 124, 138
Maisto, S. A., 32, 48, 123, 125, 139
Makela, K., 34, 35, 36, 46, 47
Maline, H. J., 182, 197
Marshall, G. L., 36, 46
Martin, E., 111, 121
Mauss, A. L., 43, 47
Mayers, Raymond Sanchez, 86, 168
McAlpine, J., 93, 106
McDuffee, D., 111, 121
McKirnan, D. J., 99, 106
McManus, 167
McNeely, R. L., 9
McNeil, John S., 51
Mello, N. K., 106, 120, 138
Mendelson, Jitt, 106, 120, 138
Messolonghites, L. A., 84, 88
Meyer, Carol H., 66, 79
Meyer, Walt, 182
Midanik, L., 32, 46, 109, 118, 120
Milgram, Gail, 150
Miller, Peter M., 6, 9
Miranda, Valetta L., ix, xiv, xvi, 21, 22, 23, 62, 64, 84, 88, 99, 100, 102, 103, 104, 106, 119, 121
Moffat, Gene H., 180, 181
Monahan, J., 9
Monroe-Scott, B., 62, 64
Moore, R. P., 123, 125, 139
Morgan, Patricia A., 9
Moser, J., ix, xvi, 32

SUBJECT INDEX